The Cornerstone

Brief

And Secrets of the Forgotten American Revolution

By Edward D. Campbell, J.D.

DEDICATION

I dedicate this work to Mr. Miles, my early American History teacher who first encouraged me into independent historical research as a student at Westport High School in Kansas City, Missouri. I also dedicate this work all to those who have encouraged me and helped me over the years to include: Mike Sparling who encouraged me for years to finish this work, to Acie DuBose who came forward in time of need, and Tracey Montesi who furnished me shelter in her home when in need as did Rayna Duenas and her mother and father, and to Lynn Olsen and Frances Ann Castro.who helped me as well as Terri L. Dean who helped me move, and the continued support from Lori Aletha, Slip and Sharon Leingang. Sharon James, Elissa Moore, Steve Strickland, Megan Mitchell, Maire M. Masco, and not to forget early support from Jim Keeling, John Ellinger, Wayne Cyphers, Lew Armstrong, Wayne Anderson, Alex Wells, Mary Jane McNulty, and many, many others, all who have helped and supported me over the years.

I take full responsibility for all the opinions expressed that are not otherwise attributed or in quotes, as well as for any errors, omissions, or editorial lapses.

2nd Printing

COVER ILLUSTRATION

TABLE OF CONTENTS

ILLUSTRATIONS

INTRODUCTION

WARNING, THE IDEAS AND INFORMATION EXPRESSED WITHIN ARE VERY DANGEROUS. They have been gathered from history, law and experience for close to forty years. They have inspired countless rebellions, the beheading or death of more than one King, overthrew other heads of state, and resulted in revolutions, including the American and French Revolutions and those that followed, loss of countless lives, volumes of blood and tears, and social and economic upheaval throughout the world. Read at your own risk. You who are super rich or powerful today, do not read and heed at your own peril. The odds as well as the facts and arguments presented within, are to your disadvantage.

If your aim is to solve the problems arising because the large disparities in wealth, power and opportunity of people, then you will need the appropriate ideology. Such legal and moral ideologies were forged more than three centuries ago, imbedded in our Declaration of Independence, adopted July 4, 1776, and doubly so in our first constitution, The Articles of Confederation, even as proposed on July 11, 1776. They were repeated twice again in our original Constitution before any amendments were proposed or adopted. Because the aristocratic rich and powerful, as groups and oligarchs, have proven they will not readily acknowledge and abide by these moral and legal principles, but would rather use their wealth and

1

power to perpetuate themselves at most other's expense, as independent, superior beings directing of the rest, it is necessary to set out the case for change in overwhelming detail. We have attempted to do that here. Hopefully this detailed information will provide all readers with the moral and legal basis, authority needed to bring about necessary social and legal changes so that we all can share a more just, equal and equitable membership in this society. again being beacons to the world.

The title is part of a description from Alexander Hamilton in the Federalist Papers promoting the adoption of the new Constitution. He called two clauses in our Constitution the Cornerstone of our republican form of government. These two clauses in the Constitution forbid both the United States and the individual states from ever granting any Titles of Nobility. These principals formed a conscious part of our framework of government from before the time of our Declaration of Independence. They were part of our first formal constitution, the Articles of Confederation, first proposed contemporaneously with the Declaration. They stood for the equality aims of the patriots already shedding their blood in revolution. Their clear desires were to limit political, economic and social inequality in the American societies that had traveled with them from Europe. The battles of Lexington, Concord of April 19, 1775 (Cover), and Bunker Hill were revolutionary struggles long before Independence. The moral and legal principles introduced by both the Declaration and the proposed Articles of Confederation were introduced in our Second Continental Congress, almost simultaneously, in June and July 1776.

A small committee drafted the Declaration, and a larger committee, composed of a representative of each colony in attendance, drafted the Articles. The "nobility" restrictions were incorporated in the very first drafts, while the States were still referred to as the Colonies. The subjects of independence and setting forth new visions of society were both the concerns of the Continental Congress in June 1776, over a year after hostilities had broken out in the American Revolution. George Washington was moving his army from victory in Boston to fight the British in New York. The clauses were adopted into the Constitution without debate and formed integral parts most of the revolutionary state constitutions of the times. While they have not been very precedent setting since, their potential is tremendous as my historical, case review and cited scholarly authorities reveal. This book is designed to be a permanent resource.

.   Unlike almost every other word and clause in the Constitution, the nobility clauses have received very little formal judicial consideration or interpretation. They have been allowed to become dusty and forgotten. They have been virtually buried for almost two hundred and forty years and not permitted to play important applications in our lives or laws. Yet, as you read this work, I hope you will find their spirit has not been eclipsed and the lessons they provide can lead us forward as a nation.

We start with a general discussion of what was considered nobility in the eighteenth century. This was a time when very formal social, legal and economic stratifications between people were considered normal and often supported by law . . . The example of Candide from Voltaire, long before the Bernstein opera, illustrates in satire of the age, the "importance" of ranking of members of society; of how they really could not find equality even in love. may somewhat overstate the case, as is required by satire, at least as applied to the English experience. But it helps set the stage for considering the eighteenth century contemporary experience and understanding. The rest of the Chapter provides a more general background for nobility as it existed in the 18th Century.

While we might think of Titles of Nobility to refer to feudal distinctions, such as Baron. Duke, King or Count, it has always had a broader meaning. Lordship aristocracy existed long before feudalism and survived it.[1] The ancient Roman aristocracy (Nobilitas Romana) consisted of three overlapping groups, or "orders". The first order were the patricii (Patricians), a hereditary caste that monopolized political power during the regal era (to 509 B.C.E.) and during the early Republic (to 338 B.C.E.). The second class were the ordo senatorius ("Senatorial Order"), which included all sitting members of the Roman Senate and their families. The final class was the ordo equester ("Order of Knights"). These groups overlapped as all

---

[1] Guy Fourquin, **Lordship and Feudalism in the Middle Ages**, translated by Iris and A. L. Lytton Sells, Pica Pres 1976 © George Allen & Ubwin Ltd. P. 13.

Patricians and Senators also held the status of Roman Knights.[2] The class of aristocracy continues to the current era, now supported by the largest and best equipped armies in the world as have been illustrated by such authors as Lundberg[3] and later students of modern aristocracy.[4] These aristocracies were not only made up of rich people, but of those who continued to preserved their wealth and attendant power for their descendants, their heirs, to use it from generation to generation, as for example the Koch Brothers today. During the early middle ages Nobility were commonly recognized by the ceremonial dubbing by the prince. But as inheritances provided social privileges and distinctions, the nobility no longer needed to be "dubbed" but merely born within the right class, and that became more and more a closed class by the thirteenth century.[5] The secret to this formation was the heritablitity of wealth , power and privilege, something recognized and enforced by the law and the power that backed the law.

In chapter 2 we turn our attention to the English experience, and English authority on the subject. Nobility was considered to include all persons from Gentlemen up to the king. All male ranks

---

[2] https://en.wikipedia.org/wiki/Roman_aristocracy

[3] Ferdinand Lundberg, **The Rich and the Super-Rich: A Study in the Power of Money** 1968.

[4] For a recent example see Chrystia Freeland, **Plutocrats: The Rise of the New Global Super-Rich and the Fall of Everyone Else** Paperback – 2013

[5] Guy Fourquin, **Lordship and Feudalism in the Middle Ages**, supra. P. 81.

were considered Gentlemen. Ladies were included, though a half a rank below corresponding Gentlemen, and without any direct political power. Only a select few of the Gentlemen were considered peers of the realm entitled to seats in the House of Lords in Parliament. The greater nobility, even including all the titled and patented nobles, formed a far larger class than just those peers seated in the House of Lords.

Following a discussion of the English experience, in Chapter 3 we turn our attention to the Atlantic Colonies of the British in north America in the 17th and 18th Centuries. We expose their experience with the effects of nobility and tendencies to class stratification. This was considerable, touching their property titles, their annual rents, who controlled the expansion of property holdings, and opportunities for enrichment and even how they might be addressed in legal proceedings. At that time the land was the primary means of production and wealth, from natural resources such as fish, game, timber and mines, to raising crops and animal husbandry. Some nobles controlled vast areas of lands in north America right up until the revolution. Land ownership and control played a vital part in the causes and expectations of the revolution.

In Chapter 4 we return to the European experience, its influence on Canada and that influence on the revolting colonies. Nobility is shown as a primary vehicle for economic participation and success in the world. The very formation of feudal dues and cultural relationships played a critical part in the formation, governance and development of Canada and many of the other north American Colonies. It would have been clear to the colonials that as the Crown tampered with the rights of nobility and revoked charters of the colonies, it could alter all the property relationships of everyone. All held land subject to escheat and reversion to the crown, or in some cases the proprietary lords. Threatened redistribution had been previously experienced. With the English victory in the French and Indian War, the west lay open to the colonials, but for the arbitrary western boundary line drawn by George III, a land grab later confirmed by the English Parliament in the expansion of Quebec and recognition of the French Civil law in that colony confirming the existing Canadian feudal-manorial system with its feudal lords.

In Chapter 5 we detail the almost universal ban on nobility contained in our revolutionary constitutions and observed in the actions of the revolutionary governments in property confiscations and prohibitions of hereditary office holding. This further emphasizes the importance of these restrictions in our constitution. We also point out the very strong English antecedents, then over a century old, that helped instruct our revolutionaries. Those words continue to instruct us on the scope of the meanings in these founding principals.

While there were no formal debates on the meaning of the Nobility clauses reported from our constitutional convention of 1789, the fear of adoption of the new constitution establishing an aristocracy was strong at the time. This is illustrated by the published correspondence of the time reported in Chapter 6. Hamilton's remarks that as long as they were excluded "the government will [not] be any other than that of the people." were not idly made. Belief that the new Constitution would not establish a new aristocracy was critical to its adoption at the time.

Chapter 7 leads us to examine the rather sparse judicial case and legal scholar's interpretation and application of these clauses. The authority that does exist makes these clauses very pregnant for potential future application. The information should help when considering the wide disparities of wealth, opportunity and private exercise of public power that exist in our own times. We may legitimately and proudly consider means for recapturing wealth and remedying some of the disparities in distribution of the community's treasures to preserve the essence of the nobility restrictions and benefit all. This is further expanded in the last chapter and epilogue to inspire further discussion for possible applications both politically and judicially.

We feel the fundamental principals expressed here have been ignored and obfuscated from time to time, and very much so today when even our government is held up to much disrespect in order to destroy its power to benefit all of us. That is why we have exposed these causes in such detail. This book is written for lawyers, historians, judges, scholars as well as for the general public. So parts may not be the easiest to read for those

just looking for entertainment. But for those who thirst for knowledge to form the future of our society, we hope your cup is being filed.

We hope copies of this work are available to all and in every high school, college and library. If you find this book useful, inspiring or with information that needs to be shared, please do so. If its revenues prove sufficient to help meet the author's shelter, sustenance, health and travel needs, we hope in the future to use all means to bring it to all the people.

Ed Campbell,
August, 2015

CHAPTER I

18th CENTURY NOBILITY

"...I think, that he was named Candide. Old servants in the house suspected that he was the son of the baron's sister and a decent honest gentleman of the neighborhood, whom this young lady would never marry because he could only prove seventy-one quarterlings, and the rest of his genealogical tree was lost, owing to the injuries of time."[6]

This lack of sufficient quarterlings starts Francois-Marie Arouet de Voltaire on one of the most celebrated satires of the eighteenth century. Quarterlings, now little more than a curiosity to most readers, were then matters of grave social and legal importance signifying those divisions on coats of arms that were indications of the number of one's noble ancestors. So when Candide found his true love's brother, after many misadventures and believing that the brother was dead, their joy of meeting was still marred by Candide's birth.

"Ah! My dear Candide," said he, "perhaps we shall enter the town together as conquerors and regain my sister Cunegonde"

"I desire it above all things," said Candide, "for I meant to marry her and I still hope to do so."

---

[6] Voltaire, Francois-Marie Arouet de; **Candide of Optimism**, edited by Norman L. Torrey, 1946, p. 1.

"You, insolent wretch!" replied the Baron. "would you have the impudence to marry my sister who has seventy-two quarterlings! I consider you extremely impudent to dare to speak to me of such a foolhardy intention."[7]

Voltaire could satirize the distinctions of rank, yet the most respected legal scholars of the time would revere such a hierarchical social system. William Blackstone published but a decade before the beginning of the hostilities of the American Revolution, that:

"The distinction of rank and honours is necessary in every well-governed state; in order to reward such as are eminent for their services to the public, in a manner the most desirable to individuals, and yet without burthern to the community; exciting thereby an ambitious yet laudable ardor, and generous emulation in others."[8]

And speaking more particularly of Great Britain

"A body of nobility is also more peculiarly necessary in our mixed and compounded constitution, in order to support the rights of both the crown and the people. It creates and preserves the gradual scale of dignity, which proceeds from the peasant to the prince; rising like a pyramid from a broad foundation, and diminishing to a point as it rises. It is this

---

[7] ibid. p. 46.

[8] William Blackstone: **Commentaries on the Laws of England**...(hereinafter BC) A Facsimile of the First Edition of 1765-69 - four volumes (Oxford, Clarendon Press), University of Chicago Press,' 1979 Vol. 1, p. 153

ascending and contracting proportion that adds stability to any government; for when departure is sudden from one extreme to another, we may pronounce that state to be precarious. The nobility therefore are the pillars, which are reared from among the people, more immediately to support the throne; and if that falls, they must also be buried under its ruins."[9]

To Great Britain that "mixed and compounded constitution" was composed to the three estates and forms of government containing the King or Monarchy; the Commons, or, according to Blackstone, the Democracy, and the 'select members' of society....'styled an aristocracy' consisting of "lords spiritual and temporal, which is an aristocratical assembly of persons selected for their piety, their birth, their wisdom, their valour, or their property...."[10]

John Adams could conflate them easily as he did in 1772: "And the Government we are under, instead of being a Mixture of Monarchy, Aristocracy and Democracy, will be a mixture of Monarchy and Aristocracy. For the lords and Commons may be considered equally with Regard to Us as Nobles, as the few, as Aristocratical Grandees, independent of Us the

---

[9] BC, vol I, p. 153.

[10] BC Vol 5., pp. 49-50.

People, uninfluenced by Us, having no fear of Us nor Love for Us."[11]

While a contemporary student of nobility at the time, Baron Von Lowhen, could, in the mid-eighteenth century, rhapsodize that "...the proper origin of nobility; indeed among all civilized nations,.." was "virtue"[12] his contemporary, David Hume, a leading 18th Century English historian and philosopher (1711-1775), could observe that in 1613, during the reign of James I of England by exercising the sovereign prerogative of the crown, that:

> "The title of baronet, invented by Salisbury, was sold and two hundred patents of that species of knighthood were disposed of for so many thousand pounds;[13] each rank of nobility had also its price affixed to it; privy seals were circulated to the amount of two hundred thousand pounds; benevolences were exacted

---

[11] **The Adams Papers**, L.H. Buterfield, Vol II p. 60.

[12] Baron Von Lowhen; **The Analysis of Nobility in its Origin With notes collected from the best English Antiquarians, and other Authors**. Printed and sold by J. Robinson, London 1754.

[13] The Baronetage of Nova Scotia (a British hereditary title, but not a peerage) had been devised by King James I of England in 1624 as a means of settling Nova Scotia. Except for Sir Thomas Temple, almost none of them came to Nova Scotia, therefore they are counted as British, not Canadian. http://en.wikipedia.org/wiki/Canadian_peers_and_baronets

to the amount of fifty-two thousand pounds; and monopolies, of no great value, were erected."[14]

Von Lowhen readily accepted the expedience of recognizing wealth by raising the possessors of wealth to the nobility;

"according to the ideas of the world, it is also a kind of disgrace to the nobility to be surpassed in splendor by plebeians, consequently, there is not the least impropriety, if the character of the person be answerable, in raising a wealthy commoner to the nobility, it is rather an increase of strength, and splendor to the order, and likewise no small incentive to extend commerce, for the accumulation of such riches, a liberal use of which, pave the way to nobility; and both these are evidently of great public advantage. The illustrious families of Nedicis, Doria, and Pallavicini, owe their nobility and grandeur to a distinguished success in commerce."[15]

While Von Lowhen passed over German, French and English examples, his English editor did not and commented in a footnote:

"A regard to wealth in point of promotion and honour, is of such long standing in this nation, that in an Anglo-Saxon law it is expressly provided that if a cearl or husbandman throve so well that he had fully five hides of his own land, a chapel, and

---

[14] David Hume: **The History of England from the Invasion of Julius Caesar to the Abdication of James the Second**, 1688) Boston 1854 Vol IV p. 432 (This work was first published between 1756 and 1761.)

[15] Von Lowhen, supra: **Analysis** pp. 287/288.

a kitchen, a house with a tower, and battlements, and had an office in the king's court, or had founded a priory, or hospital, that then he was entitled to the rights of a thane;' that is, he had the privilege of sitting in the Wittenagemot, or general assembly, he had the greatest respect and regard paid to him, and his life in the general estimation was valued at a higher price, being raised from 200 to 1200 shillings. And if afterwards this new created thane, by commendable means, made any considerable augmentation of his possessions he was raised to the dignity of an earl; likewise a merchant who made three voyages on the sea, and had thus acquired a competent fortune was made a thane.[16]

Even in ancient British society, nobility was, even in law, recognized as a badge and privilege of wealth.

So pervasive was the system of dividing people into two ranks, the aristocracy and the plebeians, that it even influenced simple forms of legal practice in Massachusetts. This was observed by John Adams as a student and young lawyer. John Adams was first admitted to the bar in 1758.[17] His diary after admission indicates frequent attendance on both the inferior and superior courts and contains notes of

---

[16] ibid.

[17] **The Adams Papers, .Legal Papers of John Adams,** L.H. Butterfield, editor in chief, L. Kinvin Wroth and Hiller B. Zobel, editors, Atheneum, 1968, originally published by Harvard U. Press, 1964) Vol, 1 p. iv, (hereinafter JA Legal).

arguments he heard before the courts as well as his own comments or questions,[18] Entries in his diary in either April or May 1761 illustrate how basic, how prevalent was the recognition and acceptance rank differentiation between men, and designation of the status of man, in pre-revolutionary America.

Under English statutes since 1413, in all original writs and some other pleadings, the writ was required to describe, in addition to the names of the defendants, their "estate or degree, or mystery" [i.e., occupation] and to give certain other information about them. The Massachusetts statutes provided that the Plaintiff's addition should also appear.[19] If the defendant's addition was not shown, the writ vas subject to abatement.20 Apparently such a legal question arose early in Adams practice and Adams made notes on it:

"Is Lawrence a Yeoman?

"It is certain, that in the modern Language both of Courts and History's, all Persons under the Degree of Gentlemen are styled Yeomen. The Gentry and Yeomanry of England comprehend all Degrees of Men from the King to the Beggar, in History, and in the modern Lawbooks a Yeoman is defined to be an ordinary common man.'

---

[18] ibid, p. lvi.
[19] JA Legal Vol. 1, p. 32, n.19.See I Hen. 5, c. 5 (1431) and for Massachusetts, Act of 3 June 1701, c 2, §I, I A&R 460.

[20] A form of dismissal.

"In Strange's Reports—It is settled over and over again, first that a Trader may be sued by the Addition of his Degree, as that of Yeoman egg. and the Writ shall not abate[21] unless he pleads another degree. Another Defendant pleaded he was a Lime merchant, and not a Yeoman. Plaintiff :demurred,[22] and the Court held, that every Man be he a trader or not a Trader, has a Degree by which he may be denoted. And that if the defendant had shown himself to be a Degree higher than a Yeoman, that would have abated the Writ, but not otherwise."

"In Modern Cases, Defendant pleaded that he was a Farmer and not a Yeoman. The Plaintiff demurred, and it was held, that if the Defendant is not a Gentleman he must be a Yeoman, i.e. an ordinary or common person.".....

"But all these Criticisms are Trash and trifling for it is settled Practice in this Court, in conformity to the late Practice at Home, to call every one of these lower sort of People, who are

---

[21] To abate a writ signifies to void or nullify it. A plea in abatement could be used to attack the technical sufficiency of a writ without reference to its merits. See JA Legal Vol 1 p. 32, a. 19 and were particularly for its use in Massachusetts, p. 71.

[22] To demur is to take an exception to the sufficiency in point of law of a pleading of a statement of fact alleged by one's opponent, that is to challenge before the court the opponent's pleadings or alleged facts on the grounds that they are insufficient to support the relief he my be requesting.

not Gentlemen and whose Occupation is not known, Yeoman."[23]

The term "esquire" to distinguish persons according to their social and political importance dates in Massachusetts back to the days of Governor John Winthrop and the 1630's.[24] Social rank even at that time followed wealth as well as birth. This could be seen in the preference given to Sir Henry Vane, (1613-1662) Puritan and son of a privy counselor, who was elected Governor of the Colony in 1638 not long after arriving in the colony in1635. Indeed poverty suffered by two magistrates was sufficient for William Hathorne (1606-1681; ancestor to Nathaniel Hawthorne) Massachusetts Deputy, to move for their removal from office in 1647, to which John Cotton (1585-1652) objected.[25]

Michael Bush, a historian who has made one of the most comprehensive modern comparative studies of the nature and extent

---

[23] **The Adams Papers, Diary & Autobiography of John Adams**, L.H. Butterfield, editor, Leonard C. Faber and Wendell D. Garrett, Assistant editors; Atheneum, New York 1964, Vol. 1, pp 208-209. This illustrates the pre-revolutionary acceptance of a stratified society in Massachusetts. As pointed out by Richard D. Brown: **Revolutionary Politics in Massachusetts**, Harvard U. Press 1970 p 5 Adams accepts as a basic tenet "...every Man be a trader or not a trader, has a Degree by which he may be denoted." For being the clever lawyer, Adams could see the practicality because defending a man sued Under the lower degree, he could get a dismissal. Not only as society stratified in Colonial America, heraldry was even utilized, Eugene Zieber, **Heraldry in America, 2nd ed.** (Bailey Banks & Biddle Co. Philadelphia 1909) Chapter IV.

[24] T. H. Breen, **The Character of a Good Ruler, Puritan Political Ideas in New England 1630-1730** W.W. Norton, © Yale University 1970, p 68
[25] .Ibid. pp 68-69, n. 105..

of noble privilege in Europe, describes nobility as forming part of and conforming to the basic legal structure of each country.

"For much of the last thousand years of European history noble privilege was not merely an expression of social superiority or of economic and political advantage. It was essentially a juridical fact, conferred or confirmed royal grant and existing not because of the laxity of the state but because of a legal provision. Thus, in failing to pay state taxes, nobles were not necessarily breaking the law frequently they were complying with. In managing to own much of the land, or to occupy the more important public offices, or to dominate parliaments, or to dispense private justice, or to avoid penalties and processes in the law, nobles were not simply asserting their power and influence; often they were exercising their legal due."[26]

Today we might cynically add in buying up the media exposure. Noble privilege was found throughout the nations and states of Europe. Indeed, even

in the Venetian republic and republican Holland could forms of Nobel privilege be found.[27] In the eighteenth century, when one referred to the rank or titles of nobility, one was not merely referring to names or

---

[26] Michael Bush; **European Nobility,** Vol. I. **Noble Privilege**" Holmes A Neier Publishers, Inc., London 1982 p. 1, (NP hereinafter) This work will be referred to hereafter as NP. It is, without doubt, one of the most extensive modern investigation of the powers, privileges and duties of European Nobility to come to the author's attention in the last almost forty years of research.

[27] NP: pp.28, 43, 57, 87-89, 92, 113, 116, 125, 135, 158,

styles of living, or the right to use or wear heraldic insignia. It referred to the economic, legal and social oligarchy. Nobility had very practical agenda as related to proprietary claims in North America by the English: For example, they might claim the quit rent, a survivor of the feudal eras, being annual rent owed to the superior lord by the inferior tenant: It survives even today in some parts of Eastern United States in the form of long term ground leases being the primary recognition of rights to possession..

Charles M. Andrews recognized in a historical text of 1919 that the appeal of quit rents influenced the seventeenth and eighteenth century nobility to seek land in North America. He acknowledged then how little we had recognized the real influence of feudal ideas in North America during these times. Gentlemen of rank sought to exercise power and achieve disparities of wealth through the exercise of rights associated with landed nobility. The feudal fantasies of John Locke (1632-1704) expressed in his "Fundamental Constitutions" merely expressed a philosophers view of the society to be promoted in the New World, based upon disparities in land ownership, control and wealth. Seigniorial rights continued to exist in England and parts of North America for their financial value and were but signs of governmental preference confirming social and economic disparities.[28]

---

[28] Charles M. Andrews, Introduction to the **Quit-rent System in the American Colonies** by Beverley W. Bond, Jr. Yale University Press (1919) pp. 18-19.

In a book published in 1726, the author gives us a fairly generally accepted description supporting the reasons for the existence of distinctions between people in England in the eighteenth century.

"Nothing in Nature could admit more Difficulty to be dispens'd with, than the Distinctions of Degrees, and Differences of Persons, which the Civil Custom, and Political Constitutions of nations, has establish'd, not only for Utility and Decency, but for the basis and solid foundation [of] Government: Nor is this a Fetch (sic) of human Policy only, but stamp'd with their **Devine Authority**, where we are commanded, <u>to give all Men their Due in their several Stations</u>. All Nations under Heaven, however drowned in Ignorance, difference in Morals, or wild in their Government, acknowledge this just and necessary Order of Submission. Tis this is the best Security of the Prince's Dignity, and the people's liberty, and is the just Poise and Balance of Government, according to the Saying of Plato: "That the Senate or Convention of the nobility and Gentry qualify'd the Heat of the Monarch and served him as a Rampart against the Insolence of the Population."[29]

---

[29] **The Laws of Honour or a Compendious Account of the Ancient Derivation of all Titles, Dignities, Offices, Etc, as Well as Temporal, Civil or Military**. Printed by G. R. Gosling, (sold by John Osborn, 1726) p. viii.

The same authority went on to describe the Gentry as (Gentlemen) being all above Yeomen and Artificers and of the class of the Civil Nobility of England.[30]

The privileges of nobility, the deference given to nobility, firmly distinguished the noble from the commoner. This distinction "frequently related to both property and person." These "privileges assumed not only that nobles and commoners... were juridically different" but so might the estates recognized as conferring noble privileges differ from the treatment of all other estates. In Europe these privileges "remained remarkably secure until the French revolution and its aftermath."[31] In the United States they were outlawed first by the Articles of Confederation even as it was initially proposed at the time of the Declaration of Independence, followed by many State Constitutions, and without reported debate in the convention, by the Federal Constitution. Charles Pinckney (1757-1824) commented on them at the Constitutional Convention, even though the proposed clauses were not part of the debate at the time.

ORIGIN

The institution...of nobility is immemorial among the nations who may probably be termed the ancestors of Britain. At the time they were summoned in England to become a part of the National Council, and the circumstances which have

---

[30] Ibid, p. 286.

[31] N1: p. 1 and n. 1.

contributed to make them a constituent Part of that constitution, must be well known to all gentlemen who have had industry & curiosity enough to investigate this subject -- The nobles with their possessions & dependents composed a body permanent in their nature and formidable in point of power. They had a distinct interest both from the King and the people; an interest which could only be represented by themselves, and the guardianship could not be safely intrusted to others. -- At the time they were originally called to form a part of the National Council. Necessity perhaps as much as other cause, induced the Monarch to look them up. It was necessary to demand the aid of his subjects in personal & pecuniary services. The power and possessions of the Nobility would not permit taxation from any assembly of which they were not a part: & the blending the deputies of the Commons with them, & thus forming what they called their parliament was perhaps as much the effect of chance as of anything else. The Commons were at the time completely subordinate to the nobles, whose consequence & influence seem to have been the only reasons for their superiority; a superiority so degrading to the Commons that in the first Summons we find the peers are called upon to consult, the commons to consent. From this time the peer have composed a part of the British Legislators...."[32]

---

[32] This is from a speech of Charles Pinckney given in the federal convention on June 25, 1787. The quote is attributed to material from Madison's notes found in **Documents Illustrative of the Formation of the Union of the American**

Thus did young Charles Pinckney display his knowledge of the origins of British nobility and privilege to the Federal Convention on June 25, 1787 and recognize the nobility was a separate class because of their power including economic power, and dependents. But he might be expected to know something of the subject. The Pinckneys were not only a prominent South Carolinian family but were members of that pre-revolutionary transatlantic society that included a number of prominent American families who had close ties and correspondents throughout the first British empire. Charles Pinckney's cousin, Charles Cotsworth Pinckney, another representative from South Carolina to the Federal Convention, had been educated at Westminster, Oxford and at the Temple in London where he completed his law course.[33] Eliza Pinckney, in the 1750's, conversed with Princess of Wales about the relative merits of suckling one's own children rather than putting them out to a wet nurse and also on the relative merits of standing children in the corner rather than whipping them as a form of aristocratic punishment.[34] Charles

States (DIF hereinafter) edited by Charles C. Tansell, G.P,O, Washington 1927, p. 268. A copy of this speech in Pinckney's hand is found in The Records of the Federal Convention of 1787 (RFC hereinafter) Edited by Max Farrand, Yale U. Press, 1911, Vol I, p 28. (Reissued in paperback). Pinckney furnished Madison with a copy of this speech which he transcribed, but apparently not with the whole of it, as Madison's note at the end indicates. The original Pinckney draft is among *the Madison papers*, and shows Madison's copying to have been accurate.

[33] Nannie McCormick Coleman: The Constitution and its Framers, Chicago, 1910, p. 457.

[34] Randolph Trumbach: The Rise of the Egalitarian Family, Aristocratic Kinship and Romantic Relations in Eighteenth Century England. Studies in

Pinckney was described in William Pierce's notes on the Federal Convention as being a young gentleman 'of most promising talents' who possessed 'a very great variety of knowledge." While "Government, Law, History and Philosophy" were his favorite subjects' he was 'intimately acquainted with every species of polite learning,...," Charles Pinckney not only spoke on nobility at the convention and later in the ratification debates, Charles Pinckney's own proposal at the federal convention was for a form of government that specifically restricted both the United States and the individual States from granting any titles of nobility.[35]

Pinckney's knowledge of Nobility displayed in this speech, or at least a good part of it can be traced almost directly to a major work first published during Oliver Cromwell's protectorate in England over a century earlier, referred to England's Commonwealth period. The Commonwealth period was a source of republican ideals well suited to teach future democrats. The idealists were sometimes referred to as levelers, or diggers, more in the tradition of the itinerant farmers occupying open space as the commons in North America. They could not afford to purchase and get title to the land from the speculators. By 1700 most of North American land came under the control of land speculators. By 1720 so much land was taken up by speculators or

---

Social Discontinuity, Academic Press-, Inc., 1973, pp. 207-208, 247.

[35]   Coleman: **Framers**. supra., pp. 454, 456.

proprietors that the poor could no longer afford to buy and ended up squatting on the land till removed and force to go further west.[36]

This authority for Pinckney's ideas was much more suitable for the social amusement but provides much European legal understanding. Pinckney gave away his source when he said in the speech quoted above;

> "Some authors are of opinion that the dignity denoted by the titles of dux at comer, was derived from the old Roman to the German Empire; while others are of opinion that they existed among th-g: Germans long before the Romans were acquainted with them,"[37]

Such :was the conclusion of Joyn Selden (1584-1654) in his "Titles of Honour"[38] Selden would have been familiar to many of those who were present when the restrictions on nobility were first proposed as restrictions on the colonies, even before they were independent. His works were at Harvard and in private libraries.[39] Fully one third of the members of the Continental Congress present in

---

[36] History 110 Dr. Olson-Raymer - **Colonial Discontent**
http://users.humboldt.edu/ogayle/hist110/colonialdiscontent.html

[37] DIF: p. 268

[38] Joyn Selden: **Titles of Honour** 3rd ed, Printed by E. Tyler and R. Holt, for Thomas Eacsett. 1672; see the second part, chapter 1, particularly parts VII, p. 240, and XXII, D. 272.

[39] H. Trevor Colburn: **The Lamp of Experience. Whig history and the Intellectual Origins of the American Revolution**; The Norton Library, 1974, see particularly library catalogues listed in appendix II.

June and duly, 1776, when the Articles of Confederation was first drafted, and others who were later signers of the Declaration of Independence were members of an Atlantic civilization, having already acquired at least some of their broader knowledge from birth, education or travel and friends, correspondents and connections in Britain and the continent of Europe. Of those who had not already studied or traveled in Britain or on the Continent another five had studied at Harvard.[40] Several others were of sufficient wealth that copies of Selden's works might be found in their own libraries. We may presume from this that not only were such concepts of nobility as could be found in Blackstone or Hume in use and were familiar with the drafters of the original nobility restrictions, but also the more detailed study that could be found in the works of Selden.

From the historical perspective, we are justified in citing Joyn Selden's **Titles of Honour** as authority for what the drafters of the Articles of Confederation and later, the framers of the Constitution could include in its determinations when they said that neither the United States nor any state could grant any titles of nobility. After pointing out that the ancient authors had undoubtedly written about the Natural and Moral Nobility, Selden observed that they also wrote about the A Civil Nobility or Gentry". He then described the quadripartite division of nobility found in the works of the school of Plato as applying to both conceptions of <u>moral</u> and <u>civil</u> nobility:

---

[40] See generally Nannie McCormick Coleman: **The Constitution and its Framers** Chicago, 1910 (first edition 1901).

27

Nobility or Gentry is divided into four Kinds. Such as are born of good and just Parents, they call Noble. If the Parents be Men of Power or Governours, their children also they call Noble. Those also we call Noble, whose Ancestors had honour either from command in the Wars, or from any of those Games wherein Crowns were rewards to the victors, And lastly, him also they call Noble that bath his own inbred dignity and greatness of Spirit. Of All which, this is the best kind of Nobility. So that Nobility hath its ground either from Ancestors eminent for Justice, or from such as were powerful, or from those that had that (other) glory, or from a mans own worth.'[41]

So Selden's four fountains of nobility are: 1) Good and just parents (inheritance); 2) Power or Governors, inheritable; 3) Ancestors success in Games and war commands, inherited; 4) Own inbred dignity of dignity and greatness of spirit, personal achievement from inherited qualities. Those who do not inherit nobility achieve it through Power or government, or by their own qualities if he or she has inbred dignity. In short, for practical purposes, for those who do not: Arise through the ranks as in the clergy = the road to nobility is power, government or inheritance.

Seiden had started his description even more simply. In discussing that great authors of ancient times had written on the subject he provided a general description of nobility when he said;

---

[41] Selden: **Titles** supra. Preface, p. (a) 3.

...."(if: you except their Sacred and Civil Offices of Employment; which frequently added to it also) the sole subordinate Title of Personal dignity, that is, <u>Gentleman</u> [or] <u>Nobilis</u>,... is literally interpreted by <u>well-born</u> with us and the <u>Dutch</u>..`[42]

Selden commences his work with a more comprehensive composition of Civil dignity:

"<u>Titles</u> <u>of</u> <u>Honour</u>, being those Various Names of Greatness or Eminency, which are the most distinguished Titles of Civil dignity are either <u>Ecclesiastical</u> or <u>Temporal</u>. The <u>Temporal</u> Titles of Honour (for we wholly omit all <u>Ecclesiastical</u>, as Ecclesiastical are either <u>Supreme</u> or <u>Subordinate</u>. The <u>Supreme</u> are either belonging to <u>Singular</u> <u>persons</u> in independent Monarchies, as <u>Emperor</u>, <u>King</u>, and what else is so Supreme according to the Customs and Languages of several Nations, or such as in Popular States and Optimacies are the Honouring titles More in one Body. The Subordinate belong to Singular Persons (those that belong to more in one body we omit also) are either such as are primarily Officiary, and only by Consequent of their Offices, Honourary, as Viceroy. Constable, Chancellor, Admiral, President, and many other also of far less dignity; or such as are Primarily Honourary and have their Offices or power (where any belongs to them) rather

---

[42] Selden, **Titles**, supra, Preface, p, (a) 2.

29

consequential or annext to their Honours, as the several titles of the Heirs or Successors apparent of Supreme Princes. that of King as it hath been attributed to some subjects, Archduke, Great Duke, **Palqrave** or Count Palatine. **Landgrave**. Prince, Marquess, Count or Earl, Visecount, **Uidame**, Baron, Banneret. and the rest of the Temporal dignities to that of Gentleman or Nobilis; or such as express only Degrees of Learning, as Doctor, Master, Licentiate and the like.

Here Selden was describing mostly titles of lordship that had survived from Feudal times. Lordship existed long before the ages of feudalism, and can be traced back to the landed aristocracy controlling the *villas*, the great landed estates dating back to Roman times. Titles merely confirmed those aristocrats with social, economic and political rights, immunities from taxes and other social obligations, and assumed duties, especially if they were profitable, within the hierarchy of Monarchal society. Existing before these times, they continue to this day throughout the world in one form or another as a consequence of wealth and power disparities. The hierarchy of landed aristocrats became the convenient local administrators for the vast Merovingian (448-741 CE) and later Carolingian empires (800-888 cE) that lacked the administrative apparatus to control their territories.. They possessed the wealth and local power to do this. But in granting them immunities and other privileges, the monarchies weakened themselves.[43] This lead to the

---

[43] See for example introduction and Chapter 1, Guy Fourquin, **Lordship and Feudalism in the Middle Ages**, Translated by Iris and A. L. Lytton Sells, Pica

fractured nature of feudal times and to such later incestuous wars as the English War of the Roses (1455-1485 cE). One might see some current similarities in the United States of states granting tax immunities, pollution control freedoms or other exemptions and/or subsidies to the wealthy and unlimited economic influence on the electoral processes and media, to establish or continue certain agricultural, industrial or extraction operations in hopes of employing its citizens and bringing economic advantages to their territories, and local entrepreneurs.

When the United States, first in the Continental Congress at the time of Independence, then by the states in many of their constitutions and through ratification of the Articles of Confederation, then by the people through their states of the United States with ratification of the Constitution, absolutely forbad both the United States and every state - from granting any 'Title of Nobility' the people and their governments required a vast change in all forms of state supported social, juridical, class, and economic structure as they were then understood. This was the statement of the fundamental principle of the social revolution that continued through the French revolution and beyond and extended back to the peasant revolts of the later middle ages.. Alexander Hamilton was not being factitious when, in arguing for support of the ratification of the United States Constitution, when he said of the nobility restrictions:

Press, 1976.

"This may truly be denominated the cornerstone of republican government; for so long as they...are excluded, there can never be serious danger that the government will be any other than that of the people."[44]

British Political Antecedents

When one reads the revolutionary constitutions of the times of our independence one develops a real feeling of their kinship to that remarkable document of one hundred and thirty years before; at the height of the republican movement in the Puritan Revolution in England. The kinship is quickly seen in this clause of that proposed:

"That all privilege or exemptions of any persons from the Laws, or from the ordinary course of Legal Proceedings, by virtue of any Tenure, Grant, Charter, Patent, Decree, or Birth, or of any place of residence, or refuge, or privilege of Parliament, shall be hence-forth void and null; and the like not to be made or revived again."[45]

---

[44] **The Federalist Papers** Oliver H. G. Leigh, ed., Washington (1901) No. 84, Vol II p. 153.

[45] William Haller and Godfrey Davis, ed. **The Leveller Tracts 1647-1653** (1944) p. 318 et seq. This remarkable document went through several editions during the time and can be found in various forms in a number of works available to the student today. In addition to the foregoing one can find it in number 26 of the **Old South Leaflets**. Student editions including Leveller works can be found in Samuel Rawson Gardner **The Constitutional Documents of the Puritan Revolution 1625-1660** (3rd revised ed. Oxford University Press reprint 1968); J.P. Kenyon **The Stuart Constitution Documents and Commentary** (Cambridge University Press reprint, 1973), and more recently A.L. Morton, ed. **Freedom in Arms** (Lawrence & Wishart, Ltd., London 1975). The author's favorite is **Puritanism and Liberty** selected and edited by A.S.P. Woodhouse,

During a quest to both discover and document the history and development of the copyright laws in both the UK and USA, that the creation of John Lilburne Research Institute took place when members of the Four Freedoms Federation discovered the genealogical and legal connections between the lives of John Lilburne (c.1614–1657) and President Thomas Jefferson (1700–1800). Thereafter interest was taken by U.S. Supreme Court Justice Hugo Black in this subject. Genie Baskir (who helped to form the Four Freedoms Federation), reports that the son of Justice Hugo Black informed her that his father even called himself a legal leveler in 1947 as he began to incorporate the ideas of John Lilburne into his Supreme Court Opinions and writings.[46]

Justice Hugo Black, cited the works of John Lilburne in his opinions, and wrote in an article for Encyclopedia Britannica that he believed John Lilburne's constitutional work of 1649 was the foundation for the basic rights contained in the US Constitution and Bill of Rights.[47]

Justice Black began championing his view that the United States Bill of Rights was applicable to the various states. Justice William O. Douglas (1898-1980) joined Black as part of the majority opinion in <u>Miranda v. Arizona</u> 384 U.S. 436 (1966). This was

---

prefaced by Ivan Roots because of its inclusion of the Putney Debates (2nd ed. J.M. Dent & Sons Ltd. 1974). We have not perused our copy of Don M. Wolf's **Leveller Manifestos of the Puritan Revolution** (1944) for this reference.

[46] http://en.wikipedia.org/wiki/John_Lilburne

[47] Ibid

written by Chief Justice Earl Warren (1891-1974) who quoted from the 1637 trial of John Lilburne as the origin of the United States Constitution Fifth Amendment.[48]

Historical studies have not only re-established the class conflict possibilities of the American Revolution but have also acknowledged the debt of the revolutionaries to English seventeenth and eighteenth century political visionary rhetoric.[49]

While we may have some difficulty in pinpointing the exact authorship of the ideas of various revolutionaries, the thoughts expressed over the preceding two centuries in Europe as well as America, and especially in England, form the fertile fields of revolutionary philosophy.

What were these historic republican principles that were readily available to our American revolutionaries. From the works of John Rushworth (1612-1690) they could read these proposals of 1647:

"That the Power of this, and all future Representatives of this Nation, is inferior only theirs who chose them

"That in all laws made, or to be made, every Person may be bound alike, and that Tenure, Estates, Chapter, Degree, Birth or Place, do not confer any Exception from the ordinary Course of Legal Proceedings, whereunto others are subjected.

---

[48] Ibid.

[49] For other surveys see R.C. Simmons *Class Ideology and Revolutionary War History* 62,204 pp. 62-70 (Feb. 1977), and Jeffrey M. Nelson *Ideology in Search of a Context: Eighteenth Century British Political Thought and the Loyalists of the American Revolution*, **The Historical Journal** 20,3 (Sept. 1977) pp. 741-749.

That as the Laws ought to be equal . . ."[50]

And in 1648:

"That in any Laws hereafter to be made, no Person by virtue of any Tenure, Grant, Charter or Patent, Degree or Birth, shall be privilege from Subjection thereto, or being bound thereby as well as others.

"That all Privileges or Exemptions of any Persons from the Laws; or from the ordinary course of legal proceedings, by virtue of any Tenure, Grant, Charter, Patent, Degree or Birth, or any place of Residence or Refuge, shall be henceforth void and null, and the like not to be made, nor revived again."[51]

And to further emphasize the importance of these propositions, they said:

"These things we declare to be essential to our just freedoms, and to a thro' composure of our long woful Distractions .."[52]

These were the Leveller principles at the time of the beheading of Charles I of England and the Abolition of the English House of Lords in 1649 and establishment of the Commonwealth two year later, and they were well understood by the American revolutionaries. As Justice Hugo Black recognized from the Supreme Court bench in 1959 in his comments on a leading Leveller of those earlier times:

---

[50] John Rushworth **Collections** (1721) *Agitators Proposals from 4 Regiments of Horse and 7 foot as foloweth*, Vol. VII, p. 859, Monday Nov. 1, 1647

[51] Ibid p. 1360

[52] Ibid p. 1361. For an expurgated copy of the agreement as available to the American revolutionaries for reference see Paul de Rapin's **History of England** with notes by N. Tindal, Vol. XII (London 1730) p. 412

"The memory of one of these, John Lilburne – banished and disgraced by a parlimentary committee on penalty of death if he returned to his country – was particularly vivid when our Constitution was written."[53]

The Loyalist opponents were close to the mark when they could say of the revolutionaries, as one did in a letter dated at Staton Island on August 17, 1776:

"It is now the Puritan's high holiday season, and they enjoy it with rapture all over the continent. Their behavior exactly assimilates the manners of the King-killing tribe during the English Grand Rebellion ...."[54]

Indeed, our own revolutionaries' animation derived from the same sources as those of their English Leveller ancestors,. This can be seen from these minutes of a meeting of the Fairfax Company in Alexandria, Virginia, when a motion was made during the revolution to elect officers annually:

"We came equal into this world, and equal we shall go out of it. All men are by nature born equally free and independent . . . Every society, all government, and every kind of civil compact, therefore, is or ought to be calculated for the general good and safety of the community. Every power, every authority vested in particular men is, or ought to be, ultimately directed to this sole end; and whenever any power or authority extends further,

---

[53]. Barenblatt v. United States, 360 U.S. 109, 134, 160 (1959)

[54] Frank V. Moore **Diary of the American Revolution** (New York 1865) Vol. I, p. 291

or is of longer duration than is in the nature necessary for these purposes, it may be called government, but it is in fact oppression In all our associations, in all our agreements, let us never lose sight of this fundamental maxim -- that all power was originally from the people. We sho d wear it as a breastplate and buckle it on as an armour."[55].

As a result of the English Civil War, the king and the House of Lords were abolished for a time (1649-1660). Charles I refused to recognize the powers of Parliament's High Court of Justice and was tried for treason , convicted, sentenced to execution and on January 30, 1649, he was beheaded. In 1660, with the return of Charles II to the throne, being a justice at Charles I's trial was not a favorable place to be and many were executed or given life sentences. Three of the justices; Major General Edward Whalley (1607-1675) and Major General William Goffe (1605?-1679?), and Colonel Richard Dixwell. sought asylum from the Crown arrest warrant, in New England where they lived out the remainders of their lives.[56] A number of prominent New Englanders had taken an active part in the Parliament's campaign against the king. .

Amongst the Roundheads (English Civil War revolutionaries) were Stephen Winthrop (1619-1652) who was the son of Massachusetts Bay Colony Governor John Winthrop, and Sir Henry Vane, who was beheaded in 1662 after conviction by the Restoration

---

[55] Kate Mason Rowland **The Life of George Mason 1725-1792** (New York 1892) Vol. I, p. 196

[56] http://patmos.tripod.com/qc/hs408p1.html

parliament of treason. He was a former governor of the Massachusetts Bay Colony.[57] Both came back from New England to support the Parliamentary cause. Other examples include William Rainborowe (1612-1673), who sold his farmstead in Charlestown to return to England, Nehemiah Bourne (1611-1690) and Israel Stoughton (1603?-1644), captain of Dorchester militia in the Pequot wars of the 1630s, who all served as officers in the Parliamentary Army under Thomas Rainborowe (1610-1648), whose regiment was packed with colonists. They were early radicals and some political levelers.[58] So we should not be surprised at the survival of equalitarian thought in that part of North America

This thought reasserted itself in New England in the time of John Pynchon, (1625 - 1701) of Springfield. Pynchon was the leading merchant and land owner in the area and a member of the perhaps two dozen merchant entrepreneurs dominant in the Massachusetts seventeenth century capitalistic society. These include, for example John Otis II (1621-1684) of Barnstable, Simon Willard (1605-1676) of Concord, Chelmsford and Lancaster, John Winthrop, Jr. (1606-1676) of Boston and elsewhere [59] Interestingly Pynchon family started with a mill (like the Canadian experience) that was needed to grind flour, and general store.

---

[57] http://en.wikipedia.org/wiki/Henry_Vane_the_Younger

[58] Adrian Tinniswood, http://www.nytimes.com/2010/07/04/opinion/04tinniswood.html?_r=0

[59] Stephen Innes. **Labor in New England, Economy and Society in Seventeenth Century Springfield**, Princeton University Press ©1983 pp 173-175

Pynchon experienced the resurrection of the equalitarian tendencies when he had occasion to call out the militia to protect settlers from Native American attacks after the Glorious Revolution, the time when James II was abandoned the throne and replaced by William of Orange and Mary in 1688. Pynchon's appointment of militia officers was not recognized and the troops insisted on democratically electing their own leaders. The Northhampton militiamen had mutinied against their appointed officers. The challenges to existing authority spread to the whole upper Connecticut valley. Every town except Springfield repudiated Pynchon's appointed officers. In direct violation of the general Court law banning local trainband election of officer, they chose their own.[60]

Direct further effrontery to the economic, class based society was the collapse of the Hampshire County Horse Troop. Membership in the horse troop required an estate valued at £100, a horse, saddle, bridle, holster, pistol and sword. This limited the membership to the better sort.' Most of the population did not possess such means. The mutiny of the upper class was a serious blow to social stability at the time. Many declared they would only serve with the foot regiment that had no such expensive prerequisites.[61]

This equalitarian undercurrent continued to be present in the colonial minds and probably inspired the drafters of the Articles of

---

[60] Innes, supra, pp. 159-164.

[61] Innes, ibid.

Confederation to include the nobility restrictions to encourage participation of the general populous in the Revolutionary Army, an such other measures, as George Washington remaining with the troops at Valley Forge. So it could be reasonably said that the equalitarian Nobility restrictions, more than any others, were necessary for, and arose out of the blood of the American Revolution.

When James Madison (1751-1836) was promoting the new Constitution to the people of New York he shared these concepts of republican government; with all power derived directly and indirectly from the people and governmental functions performed by persons holding offices at the pleasure of the people for limited times. He referred to these restrictions on nobility as part of the Constitution's guarantee to protect these principles on behalf of the people:

> "Could any further proof be required of the republican complexion of this system (the proposed Constitution then under attack as aristocratic), the most decisive one might be found in its absolute prohibition of titles of nobility, both under the federal and state governments: and in its express guarantee of the republican form to each of the latter."[62]

---

[62] **The Federalist** No. 39 Oliver H. G. Leigh, editor, 1901, Universal Classics Library, Vol I, p. 259

CHAPTER II
CLASS AND ECONOMIC DISTINCTION IN ENGLAND

Nobility in the eighteenth century had social, economic and at times definite legal connotations but cannot be generalized as a clearly defined, precisely identified, species of people. The English peers no longer formed a truly separate class but were part of a larger oligarchic-aristocratic class that included the gentry and most professional men. Men such as Washington, Adams, Hamilton and Jefferson would have felt generally at home among such a class. For example, Benjamin Franklin socialized with many of them in England at the **Hell Fire Club**.[63]

For the century following the Glorious Revolution of 1688, English society had maintained a degree of "placid stability." It was partially democratic in its law making processes and partially aristocratic. Its courts were known as incorruptible and its degree of democratic freedom, individual liberty and its underlying hypothesis of equality before the law was, as foreign observers noted, the most advanced in Europe. Its constitution preserved all from dangerous tendencies of democracy, aristocracy and monarchy, while maintaining all of these in a theoretical balance that formed the base of the much admired English Constitution of that period.[64]

---

[63] Mannix, Daniel. **The Hell Fire Club.** London: Simon and Schuster, 2001. http://en.wikipedia.org/wiki/Hellfire_Club

[64] G.E. Mingay **English Landed Society in the Eighteenth Century**, Routledge Kegan Paul Ltd., 1963, p. 259 et seq.

There were separations of class in England in the eighteenth century based on differences of family, income, holdings, position and place, education and all bolstered by affiliation with religion and party. The bed-rock of society first grounded on family and then on religion.[65]

In 1688 Gregory King estimated the population of England based upon family households. For example, the household of a temporal peer would include forty on the average. But while the family might remain central to society of our revolutionary times, its character had changed. The live-in retainers had become day laborers, the servants were no longer eating below the salt at the master's table, but below the stairs in a separate room. People were no longer being divided only according to the hierarchies of spirit and function but also in relation to space and visibility and all of this occurring during the increase of their numbers.

In England during the eighteenth century the old landed families appeared to exclude newcomers from their ranks more than at any other time in history.[66] The development of social-legal gradations in England had by our revolutionary times crystalized into a multitude of finely differentiated. ranks. A sharp line was drawn between the ranks of gentlemen and above and all below the rank of gentlemen. These distinctions had social, economic and functional connotations that are not easily outlined by the broad brushes of

---

[65] T.S. Ashton: **An Economic History of England: The Eighteenth Century**, (Methven & Co. Ltd., London, reprint 1955) p. 18_19

[66] Derek Jarrett: **England in the Age of Hogarth** (1974) (Paladin 1976) p. 89

nineteenth and twentieth century political thought. Jarrett, for example, could differentiate the lower from the upper order of mankind (it was a man's world) on the basis of the former being the producers while the latter were the consumers. [67] But while this observation might be helpful in some ways, it could also lead us to fail to consider that thoughtful people of that time considered many a day laborer, the constant potential vagabond, as an economic burden on society. He was not considered productive enough to pay his own way.

If America had experienced an aristocracy with separately established legislative and judicial functions, coupled with such restrictions of mobility of the lower orders as the English poor laws represented, and could be envisioned from restrictions on westward expansion as foreseen in the Quebec Act (14 Geo. III c. 83), given the natural differentiations as existed on both sides of the Atlantic, and perhaps a more unified nationalized religion, it would have been difficult to distinguish the water separated Anglicized societies at the time of our revolution. America certainly had the fundamental ingredient of the English class society, the gentleman. This was that species of Englishman who were equivalent to the lesser Continental nobility. [68]

In a book published in 1726 the author gives us a fairly generally accepted description concerning the reasons for the

---

[67] Jarrett, ibid p. 93.

[68] Jarrett, ibid p. 93.

existence of distinctions of people in England in the eighteenth century. They provide not only for social utility and decency, bur provide the basis and solid foundation of government.[69]

This same authority went on to describe the Gentry as (Gentlemen) being all above Yeomen and Artificers and of the class of the Civil Nobility of England.[70]

John Adams, a keen American observer of the pre-revolutionary eighteenth century could reach the same generally accepted conclusion.

> It is certain, that in the modern Language both of Courts and History, all Persons under the Degree of Gentlemen are styled Yoemen. The Gentry and Yoemanry of England comprehend all Degrees of Men from the King to the Beggar, in History, and in the modern Lawbooks a Yoeman is defined to be an ordinary common man."[71]

---

[69] **The Laws of Honour or a Compendious Account of the Ancient Derivation of all Titles, Dignities, Offices, Etc, as Well as Temporal Civil or Military**. Printed by G.R. Gosling, (sold by John Osborn 1726) p. viii

[70] The Laws of Honour... ibid, p. 286

[71] John Adams, April 3, 1761, L. H. Butterfield ed. **The Adams Papers, Diary. Autobiography of John Adams** (Atheneum, originally published by Harvard U. Pr., New York 1964) Vol. I, p. 208. This particular page from Adams diary illustrates the fundamental acceptance of stratified society in Massachusetts in the eighteenth century as pointed out by Richard D. Brown **Revolutionary Politics in Massachusetts** (Harvard U. Pr. 1970, Norton Library 1976) p. 5. Adams accepts as a basic tenet "... every Man be a trader or not a trader, has a Degree by which he may be denoted." For being the clever lawyer Adams could see its practicality for if a man were sued under the wrong and lower decree, he could get a dismissal. (**Adams Diary** April 30, 1761.) Not only was society stratified in Colonial America, heraldry was even utilized, Eugene Zieber **Heraldry in America**, 2nd ed. (Bailey, Banks & Biddle Co., Philadelphia 1909)

In England there were a couple of hundred contemporary members of the peerage during the part of the eighteenth century preceding the revolution. The English lords temporal could be distinguished by their hereditary status and the lords spiritual held office through their corporate connections. But as a whole, to the outside viewer, they formed but part of a larger class. Possible establishment of spiritual lords (bishops with secular authority) in America also was a cause for our discontent with England.

The overall social structure remained fluid enough, even if the proof were confined to the exceptional cases. There was some vertical movement between classifications in either direction, but not sufficient to destroy the social utility of various classifications that lasted in use into the twentieth century.

True, the English peerage did enjoy a few privileges such as belonging to the exclusive club of the House of Lords. That membership was their most important privilege. They were also free from arrest in civil cases and process for contempt of court could not be served against them.[72]

Lords could bring complaints against commoners in their own court, the House of Lords, for breach of their privileges such as in

---

Chapter IV

[72] **Halsbury's Laws of England** (Third Ed.) Sec. 514, p. 250-251. See also M.A.R. Graves *Freedom of. Peers from Arrest*, 21 AM.j.L.Hist. 1 (1977)

45

poaching cases and to try trespasses.[73]   They also enjoyed special privilege against Scandalum Magnatum.[74]

Some of the most detailed national analysis of the peers arose as a result of the English Peerage Bill of 1719. This proposed to increase but set a limit on the number of English and Scottish Peers in the House of Lords and to make the Scottish elected Peers' positions hereditary. According to opponents, this would have made the House of Lords the dominant oligarchy in the state.[75]

However, the bill failed passage and the nobility in England did not become a closed class oligarchy but remained open. Thus in truth it was hard to distinguish the nobility of the peerage from the rest of the affluent classes in England whose members continually

_____

[73] **Albion's Fatal. Tree. Crime and Society in the Eighteenth Century England** (Pantheon Books, 1975); Douglas Hay, *Poaching and the Game Laws on Caneock Chase,* p. 230 esp.n.4. These studies and that of E.P. Thompson **Whigs and Hunters, the Origin of the Black Act** (Pantheon Books, 1975), 1975) throw considerable new light on the eighteenth century English social background that would be interesting also to students of search and seizure rights and the rights to own and bear arms as well as general rights of accused.

[74] **Blackstone's Commentaries** ...., Vol. 1 p. 401 citing 3 Edw. 1 c 34, 2 Rich.IIst 1.c.5 12 Ric.II c11 (see note 15 for edition used) Scandalum Magnatum were words spoken in derogation of a peer, judge or other great officer of the realm for which an action would lie. The offense has not existed in this country since the Revolution: State v Shepherd,117 Mo. 205, 76 S.W. 79, 99 Am. St. Rep. 624

[75] See **The British Aristocracy and the Peerage Bill of 1719**, John F. Naylor, Editor (Oxford University Press, 1968) and **Blackstone's Commentaries** ...., Vol. I p. 157-58. See also Basil Williams **The Whig Supremacy 1714-1760**, 2nd Edition (Clarendon Press 1974 Reprint) p. 131.

intermingled through commerce, finance, appointments and intermarriage. [76]

The fear of the closed oligarchy was raised again at mid-century when Parliament tried to cure the ills of Fleet marriages that scandalized the times. One opponent to the marriage bill of 1753 predicted that the delay and publication of the bands would enable the House of Lords to close its ranks to commoners previously open through marriage and thus tend to destroy the balance in the constitution.[77] The bill passed but apparently had no more permanent effect on the mating desires represented by social breeding than we may presume existed before its enactment.

Of course the colonists, especially those who depended on hunting and fishing, had rights to be concerned after the Black Act in England preferring the aristocracy. They had been shown what could be done to their asperations by the actions of George III summarily cutting off the western lands and rivers in 1763.[78] As repeatedly recognized in the colonial charters, the crown was the fountainhead of

---

[76] For an interesting example of this process see Charles Wilson's **England's Apprenticeship** 1603-1763 (Longman Group Ltd. 1965, 1975 impression), p. 174-75) concerning the rise of Jack Childs' family.

[77] Jarrett, **England in the Age of Hogarth**, p. 119. One night marriages were causing a scandal as they were often possibly legal, meaning they were not limited to one night, easy to fall into under the dubious influence of the moment but difficult and expensive to extricate oneself from once done.

[78] E.P. Thompson **Whigs and Hunters, the Origin of the Black Act** (Pantheon Books, 1975) supra. http://avalon.law.yale.edu/18th_century/proc1763.asp

all fishing and probably hunting rights in North America, [79]

[79] Georgia, "fishing" http://avalon.law.yale.edu/18th_century/ga01.asp; Main, 1622. "fishings, hunting, hawking, fowling, http://avalon.law.yale.edu/17th_century/me01.asp; Maine1639 "Fishe as Whales Sturgeons or any other either in the Sea or Rivers and alsoe All Rovaltyes of Hawkeing Hunting Fowleing Warren and Chases" http://avalon.law.yale.edu/17th_century/me02.asp; Maine1662 "fishings hawkings hunting and cowling and all other royalltyes proffitts commodityes and hereditaments" http://avalon.law.yale.edu/17th_century/me03.asp; Maine1674 "waters Lakes dishings (sic) Hawking hunting and fl owling (sic Fowling?) and all other royalties profits Commodities and Hereditaments" http://avalon.law.yale.edu/17th_century/me04.asp; Maryland 1632 "Fishings of every kind of Fish, as well of Whales, Sturgeons, and other royal Fish, as of other Fish," http://avalon.law.yale.edu/17th_century/ma01.asp; Charter of New England, 1620: "Fishings" http://avalon.law.yale.edu/17th_century/mass01.asp; Charter of New Plymouth. Fishings" http://avalon.law.yale.edu/17th_century/mass02.asp; Charter of Massachusetts Bay: 1629, "fishing" http://avalon.law.yale.edu/17th_century/mass03.asp; Charter of Massachusetts Bay - 1691, "Fishing" http://avalon.law.yale.edu/17th_century/mass07.asp; Grant of the Province of New Hampshire to Mr. Mason, 22 Apr., 1635: "Fishing" http://avalon.law.yale.edu/17th_century/nh05.asp; Grant of the Province of New Hampshire to Mr. Mason, 22 April 1635, By the Name of Masonia. "fishings hawking hunting & fowling & all other Royaltyes Jurisdicc'ons privileges preheminence proffitts com'odityes & hereditaments wtsoever " http://avalon.law.yale.edu/17th_century/nh04.asp New Jersey 1674: "fishings, hawking, hunting, and fowling, and all royalties, profits, commodities, and hereditaments whatsoever:" http://avalon.law.yale.edu/17th_century/nj04.asp; New York: Charles II's Grant of New England to the Duke of York, 1676 - Exemplified by Queen Anne; 1712 "fishings, hawkings, buntings (sic)and fowling; and all other royalty's, profits, commodities and hereditaments to said several islands, lands and premises" http://avalon.law.yale.edu/18th_century/nj14.asp; Pennsylvania 1681: "fishing of all sortes of fish, whales, Sturgeons, and all Royall and other Fishes, in the Sea, Bayes, Inletts, waters, or Rivers within the premisses, and the Fish therein taken" http://avalon.law.yale.edu/17th_century/pa01.asp; Rhode Island, 1663: ffishing" http://avalon.law.yale.edu/17th_century/ri04.asp; Virginia Charter, 1611: "Fishings" http://avalon.law.yale.edu/17th_century/va03.asp; Carolina, 1663: "fishing of all sorts of fish, whales, sturgeons and all other royal fishes in the sea, bays, islets and rivers within the premises, and the fish therein taken"

including the Great Lakes, Mississippi and its tributaries.

The titles of the temporal peers were Duke, Marquis, Earl, Viscount, Baron and, presumably, Baronet. Fear of the establishment of the last order in the colonies played some part in the preludes to the Revolution. Most of the armorial families then in England were not of ancient ancestry, but were families who could trace their arms back one to two hundred years. Indeed, for all practical purposes, the English peerage of the eighteenth century was indistinguishable from the aristocracy and the gentry.[80] It was intimately involved in and dependent upon the practices of position, placement and pensions. It was the highest natural rank of a socially conscious society.

This somewhat amorphous species, in Blackstone's description, was divided into some sixty-six hierarchic phyla from the top gradation of the King's children and grandchildren to Gentlemen at the bottom,[81] all apparently part of that broader category of the greater and lesser nobility. This was made up of all people above Yeomen, Tradesmen, Artificers and Laborers. Possibly dear to the hearts of Professionals, Doctors (in the three learned professions) and Esquires

---

http://avalon.law.yale.edu/17th_century/nc01.asp; and 1665 ;
http://avalon.law.yale.edu/17th_century/nc04.asp;

[80] Albert Goodwin, ed. **The European Nobility in the Eighteenth Century** (Harper Torchbooks, 1967); H. John Habakkuk, **Marriage, debt, and the estates system: English landownership 1650–1950** (Oxford: Clarendon Press, 1994)..

[81] **Blackstone's Commentaries of the Law of England** (1765) Edward Christian Edition, Philadelphia 1825 Book I, p. 430.

ranked above Gentlemen and each was entitled to some opaque degree of preferment and special dress for court occasions.[82]

The mechanisms of government were in the hands of the aristocracy and gentry.[83] And to our keen eyed American diarist, John Adams, it was all one as far as the American Colonists were concerned as he pointed out in a springtime oration prepared for delivery in Baintree, Massachusetts, in 1772:

> "If K(ing), Lords and Commons, can make Laws to bind Us in all cases whatsoever, the People here will have no Influence, no Check, no Power, no Control, no Negative.
>
> "And the Government we are under, instead of being a mixture of Monarchy, Aristocracy and Democracy, will be a Mixture only of Monarchy and Aristocracy. For the Lords and Commons may be considered equally with Regard to Us as Nobles, as the few, as Aristo- cratical Grandees, independent of Us the People, uninfluenced by Us, having no fear of Us, nor Love for Us."[84]

Just because there were families with peerage whose armorial bearings conferred social prestige, one student of the subject pointed out that they did not thereby receive exclusive privileges in taxation, of law, ownership of land, entry into the army or church, nor were

---

[82] For a close contemporary instructional example see **The Book of Ranks and Dignities of British Society lately attributed in the press to Charles Lamb** (1805) with an introduction by C.K. Shorter (Jonathan Cape Ltd., London 1924).

[83] J. H. Plumb **The First Four Georges** (Little, Brown & Co., Boston, Toronto 1975) p. 15 for example of such an opinion

[84] **The Adams Papers**, supra Vol. II, p. 60

they barred from trade or industry. These noble families were not distinguishable from their neighbors through "specific and identifiable privilege."[85]

It was recognized by the American revolutionary generation that there was no great cleavage between the English nobility. The merchant, Jonathan Sewall, the Tory writing as Massachusettensis in response to John Adams Novanglus could say in January, 1775:

> "In some countries, a merchant is held in contempt by the nobles; in England they respect him. *He rises* to high honors in the state, often contracts alliances with the first families in the Kingdom, and noble blood flows in the veins of his posterity."[86]

Unlike much of the Continental European nobility, the nobility of England had by the eighteenth century lost its particular attachment, to the land.[87] Blackstone observed this disconnection from original foundations in 1765.

> "I shall next consider the manner in which they (nobility) may be created. The right of peerage seems to have been originally territorial: that is annexed to lands, honours, castles, manors and the like, the proprietors and possessors of which were (in right of those) allowed to be peers of the realm, and were summoned to parliament: and, when the land was alienated, the' dignity passes with it as appendant . But afterwards, when

---

[85] Habakkuk, supra, see also note 8

[86] John Adams and Jonathan Sewell **Novanglus and Massachusettensis** Reproduction of 1819 edition (Russell & Rusell, 1968) p.160.

[87] **Blackstone's Commentaries ....** Vol. I p. 400.

alienation grew too frequent, the dignity of the peerage was confined to the lineage of the party enobled, and instead of territorial became personal."[88]

Thus the English recognized the ultimate powers and wealth exercised by the person, not the trappings of his property, in the scheme of national power.

Nobility in the eighteenth century differed from country to country. On the Continent the nobility might be clearly distinguished by privileges in land or of taxation or even by being barred from trade and industry. But the French eighteenth century nobility had been advised to branch out from their landed revenues into trade and manufacturers.

Although a ringing indictment of hereditary majestry and a frontal assault on nobility might lie in abeyance from the restoration of the Stuarts to Tom Paine's Common Sense, the ideal of equality continued to be espoused and the *American* Revolutionaries had excellent English teachers such as the authors in **The Independent Whig** and **Cato's Letters**. These works of John Trenchand and Thomas Gordon went through numerous eighteenth century editions on both sides of the Atlantic and formed the mine for such American works as John Livingston's **The Independent Reflector**.[89] In an

---

[88] Ibid

[89] David L. Jacobson, editor; **The English Libertarian Heritage from the Writings of John Trenchard and Thomas Gordon in The Independent Whig and Cato's Letters**. (Bobbs_Merrill Co., The American Heritage Series 1965) see especially p. liii

excerpt of a 1720 piece in **The Independent Whig** we may appreciate a typical example of this rhetoric concerning espoused natural social condition:

"...(A)s to political Privileges, all Men *are born* equal; and consequently, that he who is no better than others, can have no right to command others, who are as good as himself; unless fo the ends of their own Interests and Safety, they confer that Tight upon him, during their good Pleasure, or his good Behavior."[90]

At times the reporters of the eighteenth century nobility are amusing in their own misunderstandings and contradiction. J. Brown, an eighteenth century Englishman, could feel the French nobility remained true to their feudal and military origins instead of soiling their hands with money in his work of 1757.[91] Completely unaware appears Mr. Brown of the Charles Pinot-Duclos' report that the "Grand Seineur" was (in 1750) now only a word of historical interest as those of gentle birth had already lost their right to look down their noses at the world. [92]

Some have maintained that a basic difference between French and English nobility could be seen from the derivation of Income with the English showing no sharp distinction between the incomes from

---

[90] Ibid p. 39

[91] John Brown, **Estimate of the Manner and Principles of the Times**, 2 Vols. 1757, 140, 203-4, cited in Jarrett, The Begetters .... p. 27

[92] Charles Pinot.-Duclos **Considerations sur les Moers** 1750 cited in Derek Jarrett, **The Begetters of Revolution, England's Involvement with France 1759--1789**, Longman Group Ltd., London 1973, p. 24

rents or from   commerce.[93]   But it has been pointed out that the French nobility were advised to enter into trade and manufacturers as early as 1750.[94]   Such also was the advice of Abbe Coyer in 1756 which received considerable attention.[95] Just as feudalism was not dead in England[96] commercialism was practiced by aristocracy in France.[97] Even the distinction of the French nobility not paying direct taxes as the English peerage did has been challenged.[98] Voltaire advanced the view that the children of the French nobility shunned trade but whether this was any more prevalent in French child aristocrats than in similar children in England may be questioned..

We can note some differences between. French and English nobility. The ability of the French landed nobility to escape some of the burden of general taxation contrasts with the English who enjoyed no such fiscal exemption other than through powers for appointment of property appraisers, not an inconsiderate matter of deference. Except in special situations as here noted, and in matters of natural social deference through familiarity, the English nobility, unlike the French noble landowners, were not so closely linked with the ***noblese de robe*** as to make it difficult or impossible for the commoner to

---

[93] Ashton, p. 21

[94] Charles Pinot-Duclos, **Considerations sur les Moers**, suprs. pp. 24-25, Cambridge : University Press, 1939 (French)

[95] Jarrett **The Begetters** ...., p. 61 citing "La Noblesse Commercante"

[96] Jarrett **The Begetters ....**, p. 117 citing George Warren of Lancashire

[97] Jarrett **The Begetters....**, p. 61 n 43

[98] Jarrett **The Begetters ...**, p. 23 n 14

obtain justice from them by legal means. On paper the English noble did not exercise despotic power over the yeomen, artificers, mechanics or laborers as the French nobility exercised over the peasants.[99]

In the eighteenth century the English aristocracy was probably the richest considered as a national class, while the French were perhaps the most ostentatious.[100] The strength of all aristocracies and reason for their recognition as separate social units, lay in the distinct controls they could and did exercise over the use of land, labor and the power of social confidence emanating from the corporate structure of society. Parts of the aristocracies cemented their corporate permanence through their ancient ties of heraldry and the power of myths, while other parts found their strengths in modern methods of land use, trade, industry, finance and professionalism.

From such reports, the English nobility would appear to have been as it was reported, a mild, somewhat open and not oppressive aristocracy prized as a necessary ingredient for the preservation of the balance within the English Constitution that guaranteed the basic rights of Englishmen.

In view of such a reasonable and useful social tool that could be utilized by Americans in developing their own future and preserving their own liberties what could those revolutionaries have been thinking about when it was proposed on July 12, 1776 to the

---

[99] G. F. Mingay, **English Landed Society**...., Ch. XI, p 21

[100] See also George Rude, **Europe in the Eighteenth Century, Aristocracy and the Bourgeois Challenge** (1972) (Praeger 1973) Chapter 5

Continental Congress that: "nor shall the United States in congress assembled, or any colony, grant any title of nobility.".[101]

The renunciation of this historical social and economic European aristocratic heritage was first formally proposed contemporaneously with the presentation and adoption of the Declaration of Independence in 1776. The very wording using "colony" clearly shows it was part of the revolution even before consideration of independence. It is important to consider the language of these early drafts in order to understand the intensity of this renunciation as well as the original intent of the framers of the later constitution of the United States, as little was changed from these early proposals until their final adoption in our present Constitution drafted in 1787.

Upon motion presented by Richard Henry Lee of Virginia on June 7, 1776 "That a plan of confederation be prepared and transmitted to the Colonies for their consideration and approbation" The Continental Congress resolved on June 11th to appoint such a committee with one delegate from each colony. Among the delegates appointed were John Dickinson for Pennsylvania and Josiah Bartlett for New Hampshire.[102] Two drafts of this work and some notes of the

---

[101] Article 4 of the first draft, **Journal of Continental Congress**, Vol. V p. 547. The Dickinson draft appears to have been actually prepared before the Declaration of Independence as that draft still uses the word colonies which was changed to states in the second draft presented on August 20, 1776 (Article VI) Vol. V. p. 675. This second draft contained the final form of the restriction as adopted in the Articles of Confederation.

[102] Other delegates on the committee included Edward Rutledge for South Carolina, Samuel Adams for Massachusetts, Stephen Hopkins for Rhode Island,

matters considered by this committee survive.[103] The final proposal was reported to Congress on July 12, 1776. These developments are crucial in determining original intent for the later adopted prohibitions on Nobility in Articles 1 sections 9 and 10 of the United States Constitution. They are contemporaneous with the Declaration of Independence and make their first appearance in this committee. Unlike the Declaration of Independence that speaks to the aspirations of the new government, with equality of man, these speak to the actual political and legal formation of such a society, the basic laws by which society will be governed. The surviving first drafts of June, 1776, were those attributed to Josiah Bartlett and John Dickinson.

John Dickinson (November 2, 1732 – February 14, 1808) had written the famous *Letters from a Farmer in Pennsylvania* and has been considered the penman of the revolution. He served at various times both for Pennsylvania and **Delaware** in the Continental Congress, living both in Philadelphia and Wilmington. He continued to argue against independence until he left the Continental Congress about July 4, 1776 without voting for the adoption of the Declaration of Independence. Yet he supported the revolution and served as a militia officer for his constituency. He also served as presidents of Pennsylvania and Delaware. He, along with fellow Confederation drafting committee man Roger Sherman, were delegates to the

---

Robert R. Livingston for New York, Roger Sherman for Connecticut, Thomas McKean for Delaware, Thomas Stone for Maryland, Thomas Nelson for Virginia, Joseph Hewes for North Carolina and Button Gwinnett for Georgia.

[103] **4 Letters of Delegates to Congress** 1774-1789, pp. 163-164 / 233-255.

Constitutional Convention in 1787 drafting our constitution. Dickinson, a lawyer, was among the wealthiest men in North America at the time of the revolution.

Josiah Bartlett (November 21, 1729–May 19, 1795) was a physician and a delegate to the Continental Congress from New Hampshire. Later he became Chief Justice of the New Hampshire Superior Court of Judicature despite not being a lawyer. In 1788 he served in the New Hampshire constitutional convention and was chairman of that group part of the time. He acted as president of New Hampshire in 1791 and 1792 and, after adoption of its constitution, served as Governor from 1791 until he retired in 1794. He served in the Continental Congress in 1775 and 1776 and was reelected to that body in 1778 serving in the committee charged with drafting the Articles of Confederation. He was the second signer of the Declaration of Independence.

The Bartlett draft provided, Article 4:

"...nor shall any Colony or Colonies nor any servant or servants [of the United States, or] of any Colony or Colonies accept any present, Emolument, office or title of any kind whatever from the King or Kingdom of G.B. or any foreign prince or state (under any pretence whatever) nor shall the (union) [United States assembled] or any Colony grant any title of nobility to any person whatsoever).

Bartlett's first draft recorded political and legal dreams of the revolution as they were understood even before independence, restricting what could be granted by the King of Great Britain and any other foreign power and then saying that similar grants, using the all encompassing term of Titles of Nobility, could not be granted by either the Colonies or the United States. The Dickinson draft adopted the same language, so there was really no dispute recorded of this revolutionary pre-independence declaration of that future law of the land.[104]

These clauses first appear on June 17, 1776.[105] John Dickinson, who refused to vote for independence, was a leader of the committee to draft a form of government. His drafts by relating to the colonies' support the clear evidence, including a year of fighting, that the revolution existed well before the Declaration of Independence and we should examine other causes for the revolution than some desire to separate from Great Britain. While recognizing a Colonial Union, the Dickinson's first surviving draft clearly envisioned a union that might still be within the British empire: (Art 5) "Nor shall the Union or any Colony grant any Title of Nobility to any person whatsoever."[106] The surviving contemporaneous draft in the hand of Josiah Bartlet reads (Art 4) "...nor shall the [union] [United States assembled] or any Colony grant any title of nobility [to any person whatsoever]" Bartlet was looking forward to possible independence.

As proposed to Congress on July 12, 1776 (Article 4) the provision read: "...nor shall the United States in congress assemble,

---

[104] **4 Letters of Delegates to Congress 1774-1789**, p. 235

[105] **4 Letters of Delegates to Congress, 1774-1789,**

[106] Supra. **Letters 4**:235.

59

or any colony, grant any title of nobility" [107]   Then on August 20, 1776, as Article VI the article appeared in its final form as proposed on November 15, 1777 that ratified by the States with the ratification by Maryland and its delegates on March 1, 1781: "...nor shall the United States in congress assembled, or any of them, grant any title of nobility."[108]

> "...nor shall any person holding office of profit or trust under the United States, or any of them, accept of any present, emolument, office or title of any kind whatever from any king, prince or foreign state; nor shall the United States in Congress assembled, or any of them, grant any title of nobility.

These are clear, absolute prohibitions on governmental action, whether by custom, precedence, law or treaty.   There can be no question that the American Revolution was fought to limit large disparities in equality, to put a limit on aristocratic inequality.   While these principals have been mildly enforced from time to time, principally through the anti trust laws, they have been largely, and for some, conveniently, overlooked and ignored.

---

[107] **Supra 5**:547.

[108] **Supra 5**:657.

CHAPTER III
NOBILITY IN THE NORTH AMERICA ATLANTIC COLONIES

One historian has commented that "[T]he English monarchs considered land in America to be crown property and granted fiefdoms to favored nobles."[109] But reading some of the other history of the times or then current literature, one could assume that nobility in North America did not exist at the time of the American Revolution. John Adams would comment on Massachusetts at the time, using the pseudonym of Novalingus, that in a letter from Governor Francis Bernard of July 11, 1764, Bernard advocated:

> "Although America is not now (and probably will not be for many years to come) ripe enough for an hereditary nobility; yet it is now capable of a nobility for life. A nobility appointed by the King for life, and made independent, would probably give strength and stability to American governments, as effectually as an hereditary nobility does to Great Britain."[110]

Carl Bridenbaugh has brought to our attention that along with the Royal Navy's action in preventing molasses trade at Newport,

---

[109] John Spencer Bassett, **A Short History of the United States** (2d ed 1924), p. 76

[110] Jensen, Merril ed. **Tracts of The American Revolution 1763-1776** (1967) p. 314

Rhode Island the second local fundamental grievance centered on the fact that:

> "Rumors were rife after 1761 that a faction of foreign-born residents, headed by Dr. Thomas Moffatt, Martin Howard, George Rowe, the Harrisons, and the Anglican associates, and supported by Governor Bernard of Massachusetts, who urged the creation of "a Nobility appointed by the King for Life, planned **an assault on the** Rhode Island Charter." [111]

But we are told by historians that nobility in the colonies was little known and titles of honor seldom recognized:

> "Few colonials were honored, William Phips, born in Main, was Knighted in 1687. William Pepperwell, of the same origin,

---

[111] Carl Bridenbaugh , **Cities in Revolt** (Oxford University Press 1971) p. 309. See also R.R. Palmer: **The Age of Democratic Revolution** (Princeton University Press (1969) vol. I, p.176; Carl Bridenbaugh,: **Mitre and Septer** (Oxford University Press, 1967) p. 250; Esmond Wright: **Fabric of Freedom 1763-1800** (Hill & Wang 7th Printing 1968) p. 76; Gordon S. Wood: **The Creation of the American Republic** 1776-1787 (Chapel Hill 1969) p. 111-112, noes 47 and 48 especially John Dalrymple's address to America. A plan to create 10 peers in the colonies by royal prerogative is located in the Franklin manuscripts and bears the date of November 17, 1770, signed by Amos Patriae, a pseudonym for Thomas Crowley – see Cecil B. Curry: **Road to Revolution, Benjamin Franklin in England 1765-1775** (Doubleday Anchor Original 1968) p. 164 n. 19. On the subject of American peerage see also Jackson Turner Main; **The Anti Federalist** (W.W. Norton & Co., Inc. N.Y. 1961) (Norton Paperback 1964) Chapters V and VI.

was made a baronet in 1746, and William Johnson, of New York, received the same honor in 1755.[112]

So why do we find so many constitutions proposing to ban and actually banning nobility, one even before the Declaration of Independence? The reason is plain. Nobility was well known in North America at the time and indeed for many years preceding the revolution and incorporated into the original charters of many colonies. These land speculating nobles were controlling some of the largest sections of land in North America, including parts of the West – cutting off or relying on colonial land claims. New England had a fear of reestablishing the proprietary-nobility claims after the Stuart Restoration (1660):

> "The relaxed control exercised by the British government during the Puritan Revolution and the period of the Commonwealth and Protectorate greatly strengthened the system of free tenure of land in New England. With the downfall of the proprietary claims in Maine and New Hampshire, both colonies passed temporarily under the jurisdiction of Massachusetts and thus seemed secure from proprietary control. But after the Restoration, when efforts were made to revive many of the earlier seigniorial grants, in order to increase the incomes not only of the crown but of members of the nobility also, there was some reason to fear lest quit-rents

---

[112] Robinson, W. A.: **Dictionary of American History** Vol. IV, p. 136. James Thurlow Adams, Editor in Chief, Charles Scribner, 1940.

be established in parts of New England. The only serious danger came from the effort to revive the claims of Mason and Gorges. The proprietary rights set up by the heirs of the former proved a source of much controversy in New Hampshire, while those of the latter were purchased by Massachusetts in 1678. With Maine finally included in Massachusetts and all other proprietary claims dismissed by the crown, the quit-rents were banished from all New England except New Hampshire. Clearly, if the proprietary rights of the crown were to be asserted in the New England colonies, the system of land tenure free from the usual feudal charge, the quit-rent, must first be attacked in its chief stronghold, Massachusetts.[113]

Vestiges of that nobility remain even today. These comments, still valid, were published almost 100 years ago:

"Many fail to realize that on our own soil, as elsewhere, democracy, free government, and a more just, equable, and humane system of law and order have evolved slowly though steadily from a state of society in which the royal prerogative, aristocratic distinctions, and some of the rules of feudal law were living realities to a large proportion of the population.

"In no single particular have the customs of the past been more tenacious and persistent than in the domain of real property, for even to-day the laws governing descent, contract,

---

[113] **Quit-rent System in the American Colonies** by Beverley W. Bond, Jr. Yale University Press (1919) p. 42.

conveyance, and tenure bear the marks of their feudal origin. It is hardly surprising, therefore, that in colonial times in America, landholding should have been essentially tenurial in character. Except in the corporate colonies of Massachusetts, Rhode Island, and Connecticut, the formula held good, *nulle terre sans seigneur,* for every acre of land was held of a lord, either the king himself, or some landed proprietor or proprietors to whom a grant had been made by the crown. Even in those colonies, though there was nothing tenurial about the way the towns distributed their lands among their own inhabitants, for the Puritans were vehemently opposed to the distinction between lord and tenant and were determined to be "supreme lords of their own lands," equal before God and the law, there was much that was tenurial in the higher relations of town and colony with the crown. The corporations held their lands of the king by a socage tenure, and though no rent was demanded by their charters, because the latter were in origin the instruments of trading companies and not of feudal lords, they might have paid such a rent had it been demanded, as Massachusetts thought of doing in 1681, when threatened with the loss of her charter. The Connecticut towns acknowledged their legal status as tenants in socage of the crown, when in 1685 and 1686 they took out formal patents of confirmation to protect their lands from reverting into the king's hands at the time of the Andros government. Thus the feudal' landed relationship, which was so widely prevalent elsewhere, had a

65

place even in these self-governing Puritan colonies, and it is incumbent on us to know something of the origin and character of a tenure by which so large a portion of the colonial lands was held.

This tenure was commonly styled free and common socage or tenure in fee-simple, the terms of which were fealty and a fixed rent. Feudally speaking, fealty was the bond between lord and man, which survived only in the oath of allegiance to the crown ; rent was the bond between the lord and the land, the symbol of territorial ownership, and was usually called the quit-rent, or sometimes—and there is an instance of this in the "Fundamental Constitutions" of Carolina —the chief rent. In addition there were other incidents, such as alienation fines and escheats. The quit-rent was originally a commutation in money of certain medieval villein obligations, such as laboring for the lord of the manor a number of days in the week and paying to him a portion of the produce of the villein's land and stock. In very early times in England, the payment of a money rent seems to have been the privilege of the class of sokemen (whence the name of the tenure), the free peasantry, who in considerable numbers survived the Norman Conquest, and as a commutation to have been applied first to those of the unfree who held "uncertainly" or at the will of the lord, that is, the future copyholders as contrasted with the freeholders. But later the quit-rent was used to designate any form of payment, which absolved or made quit the tenant, whether vassal, freeholder, copyholder, or leaseholder, in respect of personal service or other similar obligation to the lord. The tenure thus evolved became the "freest" of all the English land tenures, and because of its easy adaptability to a changing land system, which was gradually throwing off its medieval fetters, was widely employed to meet the need of a simpler and more flexible method of acquiring landed property. The strictly feudal tenures, knight's service, frankamoin, grand serjeanty, and petty serjeanty, had become formal and rare by the seventeenth century and the first named was becoming obsolete long before its abolition by the Restoration Parliament in 1661, so that socage tenure was all but universal in the British world during our colonial period.' As there were no copyholds in America. [114]

Seigniorial rights were exercised in all colonies except New England at the time of the American Revolution. The royal order in 1683 that annexed Pemaquid to Massachusetts, illustrates the general fact that the grant of a propriety in America carried with it the right to impose a quit-rent as a source of revenue for the grantee. [115]

The quit-rent was established with varying success in all the American colonies except those of New England. Throughout the

---

[114] Charles M. Andrews, Introduction to the **Quit-rent System in the American Colonies** by Beverley W. Bond, Jr., Yale University Press (1919) pp. 13-16

[115] Bond, p. 112, Instructions to Governor Andros, July 1, 1674, and to Governor Dongan, January 27, 1683, N. Y. Col. Does., III, 216-217, 331-334.

colonial era the proprietaries retained the right to reserve such dues in the Jerseys, in Pennsylvania including the Lower Counties, and in Maryland. The crown collected the quit-rents in New York after the Duke of York became king; in Virginia after the charter was annulled in 1624; in the Carolinas after the purchase from the proprietaries in 1729; and in Georgia after the surrender by the trustees in 1752. In the West Indies, too, the crown either granted the soil to proprietaries, or retained it in its own bands. In either case there was a reservation of quit-rents, except in Barbados and the Leeward Islands, where they were waived in favor of the more productive four and a half per cent. export duty. A quit-rent was reserved also in Nova Scotia after the conquest from the French, and the proclamation of 1763 specifically required that such a feudal dues to the crown should be included in all grants in Quebec, in East and West Florida, and in Grenada.' Reserved therefore in by far the majority of the colonies both royal and proprietary, the quit-rent became an important feature of the land system in the American colonies. [116]

They were the source of substantial revenue to some in Colonies, a nuisance to others, and often hard to collect:

> Quit-rents were either real or nominal, either an actual sum of money or a mere token of lordship, the rendering of which was evidence of the freeholder's inferior title. Proprietors, such as the Baltimores, the Penns, the Duke of York, or the corporation of the city of Albany, tendered Indian arrows or beaver skins,

---

[116] Ibid, Bond pp.32-33.

and occasionally those lower in the scale made similar payments, as of a red rose for a manor in Pennsylvania or a silver shilling for a whole barony in South Carolina.' But more often the quit-rents had a real money value and were a source of income to those who owned the land. The proprietors of the Jerseys and the Carolinas paid or should have paid (for they were generally in arrears) a goodly number of marks or nobles ; while the settlers who occupied the soil met their obligations in sums ranging from a penny an acre to as low as two shillings and six pence a hundred acres and sometimes less. In no case was the quit-rent a heavy financial burden to the colonist though the requirement, often imposed, that the payment be made in silver rather than produce, was difficult to meet, owing to the scarcity of hard money. It was nota rent, as we define the term, bearing a value proportionate to the worth of the land; it was a compounding for service, the ,rendering of a fixed annual sum, which remained the same whether the price of land rose or fell. Many a farmer, in Virginia, for example, who was a leaseholder not a freeholder, a tenant, that is, possessing no fee of the soil, paid a rent to his landlord as well as a quit-rent to the king. The total amounts received from the quit-rents were often considerable, as they were bound to be in a country where land was plentiful and grants in fee were many, and they added appreciably to the revenues of the Baltimores, the Penns, Lord Fairfax, and Lord Granville. The quit-rents of Virginia were sufficiently large to find a place in the estimates of the British

69

Exchequer. But the sums were always affected by the refusal of the colonist to pay, by the difficulties of collection, and by the large outstanding arrears that everywhere accumulated. The proprietors of the soil in New Hampshire and the Jerseys had almost nothing to show for their titles, and the crown in New York netted very meager returns from the quit-rents of that province. Taking the British colonies as a whole, there were many instances in which the system worked so badly that the obligation to pay remained little more than a dead letter.[117]

In post-feudal times, quit rents have continued to be imposed by some governments, usually attached to land grants as a form of land tax. [118]

Dominion of New England

The Dominion of New England is instructive on the powers of the nobility, in this case the grand noble, James II, King of England It was a short lived affair from 1686 until James II left England in 1688, having little permanent administrative or legal influence in North America other than permitting the Church of England to operate in Massachusetts.

The Dominion encompassed a very large area (from the Delaware River in the south to Penobscot Bay in the north), composed of present-day Maine, New Hampshire, Vermont,

---

[117]   Beverly W. Bond, Jr. supra. **The Quit Rent System** pp17-18.

[118] http://en.wikipedia.org/wiki/Quit-rent:

Massachusetts, Rhode Island, Connecticut, New York, and New Jersey.

Charles II repeatedly sought to change the behavior of the Massachusetts governing elite, but they proved recalcitrant, resisting all substantive attempts at reform. In 1683 legal proceedings were begun to vacate the Massachusetts charter. It was formally annulled in June 1684.

Edmond Andros dealt a major blow to the colonists by challenging their title to the land. Unlike England, the great majority of Americans were land-owners. Taylor says that because they "regarded secure real estate as fundamental to their liberty, status, and prosperity, the colonists felt horrified by the sweeping and expensive challenge to their land titles."[119]

Andros had been instructed to bring colonial land title practices more in line with those in England, and introduce quit-rents as a means of raising colonial revenues.[120] Clearly, if the proprietary rights of the crown were to be asserted in the New England colonies, the system of land tenure free from the usual feudal charge, the quit-rent, must first be attacked in its chief stronghold, Massachusetts. [121]

---

[119] Taylor, Alan, **American Colonies: the Settling of North America**, Penguin Books, 2001. p 277.

[120] Barnes, Viola Florence. **The Dominion of New England: A Study in British Colonial Policy** (1923) p.176.

[121] **Quit-rent System in the American Colonies** by Beverley W. Bond, Jr. Yale University Press (1919) p. 42.

The titles issued in Massachusetts, New Hampshire, and Maine under the colonial administration often suffered from defects of form (for example, lacking an imprint of the colonial seal), and most of them did not include a quit-rent payment. Land grants in colonial Connecticut and Rhode Island had been made before either colony had a charter, and there were conflicting claims in a number of areas.[122] Upon the urging of Edmond Randolf, then collector and surveyor of the customs for all New England[123] and others, the Massachusetts Charter was forfeit in 1684.

The third governor of the Dominion of New England, Edmond Ardros took charge 1n 1686. Evidently Andros was required to make a quit-rent a condition of confirmation for all lands held in Massachusetts, and after other charters in New England had been annulled to establish quit-rents in similar fashion elsewhere.[124]

Andros approach was divisive, as it threatened any landowner whose title was problematic. Some landowners went through the confirmation of their titles process, but many refused, since they did not want to face the possibility of losing their land. Many viewed the process as a thinly veiled land grab. The Puritans of Plymouth and Massachusetts, some with extensive landholdings, resisted. [125]

---

[122] Barnes, p. 182, 187.

[123] Bond, p. 44,.
http://www.britannica.com/EBchecked/topic/491019/Edward-Randolph

[124] Bond, p.44

[125] Barnes, pp. 189–193.

Because the existing land titles in Massachusetts had been granted under the now-vacated colonial charter, Andros had recently declared them to be void, and required landowners to recertify their ownership, paying fees to the dominion and becoming subject to the charging of a quit-rent.

Andros attempted to enforce certification of ownership by issuing *writs of intrusion.* Large landowners who owned many parcels contested these individually, rather than recertifying all of their lands. The number of new titles issued during the Andros regime was small: 200 applications were made, but only about 20 of those were approved. [126]

Connecticut presented similar problems.

This Puritan idea of a land tenure free of all feudal incidents and restraints completely controlled the Connecticut people from the beginning. In 1643, George Fenwick, one of the English lords and gentlemen who were planning to find a refuge in Saybrook in case affairs in England went against the Puritans, having failed to sell to the Connecticut colony the rights of the patentees, proposed to levy a quit-rent on every acre of improved land, but found that the occupiers of the soil would not listen to the suggestion, for, as he ironically complained, "we must all here be independent and supreme lords of our own land.'" A year later, despairing of raising a revenue from a quit-rent, he disposed of the lands controlled by the patentees at the mouth of the river for a certain sum of money, to be paid in the form

---

[126] Barnes, pp. 199–201.

of dues that he was to collect for the ensuing ten years. These dues were probably much heavier than a quit-rent would have been, and much less easily evaded, and show that to Connecticut the issue was not one of money but of tenure—a tenure free from the obligations that rested on freehold and copyhold at home.[127]

Free tenure of land was assured by the Connecticut Code of 1650 forbidding all feudal incidents,'supported by the charter of 1662, which vested all rights to the soil in the governor and company for the benefit of the freemen.[128] The charter of **Rhode Island** followed suit "in 1663 reflecting the influence of the Massachusetts land system in preventing the establishment of quit-rents in neighboring colonies" [129]

Maryland

Nobility, seigniorial rights were exercised in Maryland by the Calverts, Barons of Baltimore and Lord Proprietors. They claimed quit rents as feudal dues owed them perpetually for the original patents they had granted as they conveyed portions of their property grant from the crown. In 1780 Maryland abolished quit rents. The rents had not been paid from 1771 to 1780 and a modern author

---

[127] Bond, pp. 39-40.

[128] **Fitz-John Winthrop to Andrew Hamilton, Letter of June 9, 1698**, Mass. Hist. Soc. Col., 5th series, IX, 193-195.

[129] Bond, p 40

estimated that if all were collected would have amounted to over $13 million would have been owed in the state 2005 standards[130]

The original crown grant of 1632 gave the Proprietors full seigniorial rights and franchises of the crown, to enjoy them as "Amply as any Bishop...within the Palatine[131] of Durham...hath... enjoyed." This meant that the Calverts were granted the full rights that the King could exercise in his Palace, full sovereign rights. The proprietors were authorized "for the good and happy government of said Province, to ...enact...Lawes...with the advise, assent and approbation of the Free-men of said Province" and "enjoy...Customs and Subsidies." [132]

In exercise of their rights the Proprietors, Lord Baltimore and his heirs, could "assigne, aliene, grant, demise or enfeoff" the lands within the Maryland grant"to persons willing to take of purchase the same...subject to such...rents as shall seem fit." The Proprietors could

---

[130] Power. Garrett: **Calvert vs. Carroll The Quit-Rent Controversy Between Maryland's Founding Families**. .(2005) http://papers.ssrn.com/sol3/papers.cfm?abstract_id=680661

[131] In Early Modern Britain, the term *palatinate*, or county palatine, was also applied to counties of lords who could exercise powers normally reserved to the crown. Likewise, there were palatine provinces among the English colonies in North America: Cecilius Calvert, 2nd Baron Baltimore, was granted palatine rights in Maryland in 1632, as were the proprietors of the Carolinas in 1663. http://en.wikipedia.org/wiki/Palatine

[132] MD Charter 21-22 (1632).

also "erect any parcels of land within the Province...into Manors."[133] Thereby the Lords Baltimore could subinfeudate tenements to themselves and create their own feudal kingdom.

After the Glorious Revolution in 1688 and ascension of their protestant magistries, William and Mary, the Roman Catholic Calverts lost their seigniorial rights as the colony became a crown colony in 1692. But they retained the proprietary lands and quit rents.

Before his inheritance Benedict Calvert converted to Protestantism and thus was enable to regain the seigniorial rights to the Province in 1715. He died the following year. Quit rents were for a time replaced by export duties, making it easier to collect, but these were repealed in 1733 and the quit rents returned. By the American revolution they amounted to over £8,000[134] a year.(estimated at over £200,000 in today's funds). One calculation estimates the quit rents amounted to about an average rate of about 1% of the value of property per annum. So feudalist nobility was strong at the time in Maryland an many current bankers would be happy with that rate of return on nothing.

The Carolinas

After Charles II ascended the throne in 1660, he awarded in 1663 as Lords Proprietors, eight of his allies with land in North and South Carolina together with quit rents. They were the Earl of

---

[133] MD Charter 5, 9, 20. (1632)

[134] Grant Power "Calvert vs. Carroll, supra. P. 17.

Clarendon (high chancellor of England), the Duke of Albemarle (master of the King's horse and captain of his forces), Lord William Craven, Lord John Berkeley, Lord Anthony Ashley (chancellor of the King's exchequer), Sir George Carteret (knight and baronet and vice-chamberlain of the King's household), Sir William Berkeley (knight) and Sir John Colleton (knight and baronet). They were granted absolute sovereignty similar to that granted in Maryland.

John Locke, drew up a fantastic feudal form of government for the Carolinas under the direction of the Earl of Shaftesbury. The proprietors issued four revisions later. The plan included provisions for nobility appointed by the proprietors, "Landgraves" and "Caziques," who would own permanently two fifths of the land. It also provided for a grand council made up of the proprietors and their counselors that would exercise executive authority in the colony, and through this control legislation. It provided for the establishment of the Anglican Church, some religious toleration, and for serfdom and slavery. The attempt to force this on the Colony was abandoned in 1690.[135]

The Carolina quit rents proved to be a matter of controversy up to the Revolution. Even when seven of the proprietors sold their claims back to the crown in 1729, John Carteret, the Earl of

---

[135] **The Fundamental Constitutions of Carolina**, John Locke (1669) http://www.constitution.org/jl/funconcar.html; R. T. Merriwether **Dictionary of American History** Vol. I, p. 316. James Thurlow Adams, Editor in Chief, Charles Scribner, 1940. See also Edward McCrady, **The History of South Carolina Under the Proprietary Government**; S. A. Ashe: **History of North Carolina.** http://www.constitution.org/jl/funconcar.html

Granville, kept his land and manorial rights to the quit rents.[136] In 1730 he agreed to give up any participation in government in order to keep ownership of his share. This share was later defined as a 69-mile wide strip of land in North Carolina adjoining the Virginia boundary, and became known as the Granville District.

The lands of the Granville District remained in the Carteret family until the death of Carteret's son Robert in 1776. Following the American Revolution, Robert's heirs were compensated in part for the loss of the lands. Two modern counties of North Carolina have been named in his honor, Carteret County and Granville County.[137] During the revolution the General Assembly declared the lands of the late Earl Granville in North Carolina were forfeited to the State of North Carolina. The Carteret heirs were awarded for the loss of quit rents by the British Commissioners appointed by Parliament to address the losses of the loyalists, but the commissioners did not redress the loss of the fee and that remained subject to litigation for years. It was a fee for land 69 miles or 111 kilometers in breadth from the Atlantic to the Mississippi River across North Carolina and Tennessee with Virginia as its northern border. This is a distance about 700 miles or a little more than the distance from London to Berlin, or close to the distance between New York and Indianapolis or San Francisco to El

Kickler, Troy L.: *North Carolina History Project, Quitrents (Colonial Period)* http://www.northcarolinahistory.org/commentary/121/entry

[137] John Carteret, 2nd Earl Granville, 7th Seigneur of Sark.
 http://en.wikipedia.org/wiki/John_Carteret,_2nd_Earl_Granville

Paso. It would have included over forty eight thousand square miles, or three million acres of land or almost one and a quarter million hectares, over three and a half times the size of the famous King Ranch in Texas, and far more valuable, dwarfing many Noble estates in Europe including many kingdoms at the time.

Few, if any of the greatest European lords, nobility, could command such an inheritable estate in Europe. If it were owned today, the owner would be a multi trillionare. The name of its pre revolutionary seigneur, John Carteret, 2nd Earl Granville, 7th Seigneur of Sark, still survives on the channel Island of Sark, subject only to the crown of England (not the parliament) and famous for its off shore banking and no taxes. It has no reciprocal tax arrangements with the United Kingdom or the rest of the world.. Its Chief Pleas (local parliament), consists of 40 tenants and 12 popularly elected deputies, presided over by the Seneschal (L. P. de Carteret). It presides over and above the duties it owes to stockholders and in decisions cannot be disputed or challenged. It is the home of two banks, (the Bank of Westminster and Midland Bank) and about 600 residents. It is a favorite international tax haven[138] and the home or resting place of who knows how much wealth.

The thirteenth clause of Charles II charter to the Carolinas of 1663 granted the proprietors the right to grant marks of favor and titles of honour so long as not the same as those granted by the crown

---

[138] http://www.offshore-manual.com/taxhavens/Sark.html

in England.[139] In 1669 the proprietors offered the Carolina's a new form of government much of which is mostly attributed to John Locke, the famous English philosopher of the time.   The whole proposal, as we have observed, was a mixture of mostly feudalism with some liberal provisions. The eldest proprietors was to have the power of a lord palatine with this right to the remaining eldest proprietor. The other lords proprietor were to hold the chief offices of the colony. The Fundamental Constitutions of Carolina, March 1, 1669[140] provided:

> "Three. The whole province shall be divided into counties; each county shall consist of eight signiories, eight baronies, and four precincts; each precinct shall consist of six colonies.[141]

> "Four. Each signiory, barony, and colony shall consist of twelve thousand acres; the eight signiories being the share of the eight proprietors, and the eight baronies of the nobility; both which shares, being each of them one-fifth of the whole, are to be perpetually annexed, the one to the proprietors, the other to the hereditary nobility, leaving the colonies, being three-fifths, amongst the people; so that in setting out and

---

[139] http://avalon.law.yale.edu/17th_century/nc01.asp Charter of Carolina - March 24, 1663

[140] http://avalon.law.yale.edu/17th_century/nc05.asp#b3

[141] Francis Newton Thorp, ed: **Federal and State Constitutions Colonial Charters, and Other Organic Laws etc.** (1909) p. 2772

planting the lands, the balance of the government may be preserved.."[142]

"Nine. There shall be just as many landgraves as there are counties, and twice as many caziques, and no more. These shall be the hereditary nobility of the province, and by right of their dignity be members of parliament. Each landscape shall have four baronies, and each cazique two baronies, hereditarily and unalterably annexed to and settled upon the said dignity."[143] ...

"Thirteen. No one person shall have more than one dignity, with the signiories or baronies thereunto belonging. But whensoever it shall happen that any one who is already proprietor, landgrave, or cazique shall have any of these dignities descend to him by inheritance, it shall be at his choice to keep which of the dignities, with the lands annexed, he shall like best; but shall leave the other, with the lands annexed, to be enjoyed by "him who, not being his heir apparent and certain successor to his present dignity, is next of blood.."[144]

The Fundamental Constitutions of Carolina did not prove to be popular and failed for want of assent by the general assembly. But even if not adopted, it is interesting in the way it limited the landed wealth, the main means of production, of the Carolina nobility (clause 13).

---

[142] Thorp supra.

[143] Thorp p. 2773

[144] Thorp p. 2774

Virginia

Virginia started in 1606 as the London Company, with a council in England and a governor in the Colony. A new charter was issued ain 1609 whereby the London council became part of the company. The first House of Burgesses, composed of twenty-two delegates, met in July, 1619, and before long the people were living under their own laws thereby initiating its first foothold on American soil of a "government of the people, for the people, and by the people." The Puritans promoting this were at odds with the Stuarts, and in 1624 the charter was dissolved under the chief feudal lord, King James I, and Virginia became a Royal Colony until the Revolution.

In Virginia, the first colony under private control that was actually set up in America, there were no quit-rents during the first few years when all property was held in common. But after the division of the land, the London Company reserved 2s per 100 acres as the usual sign of proprietary ownership. Since this quit-rent was not pay-able until seven years after a patent had been issued, it did not become due before 1624, when the crown took over the rights of the London Company.' Throughout the greater part of their history, therefore, the quit-rents of Virginia were enforced as feudal dues payable to the crown rather than to proprietaries.[145]

Not all of Virginia remained a Royal Colony as a large part, known as the Northern Neck Land was developed as a

---

[145]   Bond, pp. 109-110.

proprietorship.   The proprietors controlled an area bounded by the Rappahannock and Potomac Rivers and stretched from the Chesapeake Bay to what is now West Virginia. It embraced all or part of the current Virginia counties and cities of Alexandria, Arlington, Augusta, Clarke, Culpeper, Fairfax, Fauquier, Frederick, Greene, King George, Lancaster, Laden, Madison, Northumberland, Orange, Page, Prince William, Rappahannock, Shenandoah, Stafford, Warren, Westmoreland, and Winchester, and the current West Virginia counties of Berkeley, Hampshire, Hardy, Jefferson, and Morgan.

Northern Neck Proprietary grant 1649 from the soon to be beheaded Charles I, covered over 5,250,000 acres or more of land eventually comprising at least 22 Virginia Counties, with three of them in what is now West Virginia. It was perhaps as large or larger than the size of the Esterhazy estates in Hungary, Austria and Bavaria, where Franz Joseph Hayden was composing and conducting at the time of the American Revolution.   The ultimate ownership of the Proprietary devolved to Lord Thomas Culpeper (son of Thomas Culpeper, one of the original proprietors) in 1688. In that year, King James II issued a new charter to him as sole proprietor. This charter greatly enlarged the original territory and defined it to the headwaters of the Rappahannock and Potomac Rivers, leading to a number of legal disputes not settled until 1745. On lord Thomas's death, The Proprietorship descended to his widow, Margaret Lady Culpeper. Eventually, all of the shares became the property of Thomas Lord Fairfax and remained in that family until after the Revolution.

The Fairfax family continued to control the waste lands and the quit-rents from sale until the revolution. The quit-rents were forfeited, but that did not result in an immediate forfeiture of the land.[146] The quit-rents were fixed rent payable to a feudal superior in commutation of services; specifically a annual fixed rents due from a socage tenants who were all the grantees of Lords Fairfax and his forebearers from the time of the grant of Charles II. The proprietorship controlled its own land office until the revolution. So in the North Neck Virginia, Nobility of the seigniorial type was alive and well until the time of American Revolution, even though the Virginia courts did operate in the North Neck. That worked well for the proprietors as courts are an expensive luxury that seldom cover their own costs.

Thomas Lord Fairfax was the only Proprietor to reside permanently in the thirteen colonies at the time of the revolution. After Thomas, Baron Cameron, Sixth Lord Fairfax, returned to Virginia in 1747, he lived at his cousin William Fairfax's home, Belvoir (now the site of Fort Belvoir), before building a home in the Shenandoah Valley. He named his small stone house "Greenway Court" and settled there permanently in 1762 until his death in 1781. In 1748 Lord Fairfax engaged George Washington to work with his survey team to survey some of his vast holdings of approximately 5 million acres between in the "headwaters" of the Rappahannock and the Potomac often referred to as the "Northern Kneck." The Privy

---

[146] <u>Fairfax's Devisee v. Hunter's Lessee</u> (1813) 11 US 603, 7 Cranch 379

Council in 1745 confirmed northern Shenandoah Valley to Fairfax, together with other lands now apart of West Virginia. These holdings, in the Shenandoah Valley, included all or portions of as many as 35 Virginia and West Virginia counties.[147]

Fairfax was an early mentor and friend of George Washington, giving him a job as a sixteen year old apprentice in 1748 helping to plat part of Fairfax's propriety across the Blue Ridge. It may have helped that George's brother Lawrence, was related by marriage to Lord Fairfax. Fairfax kept a low profile during the revolution. He was the only peer living permanently in North America at the time, as the claim of William Alexander, a highly praised American general in the Revolution living in New Jersey, that he was the "Earl of Stirling" was never successful. Other peers who held offices in the Colonies from time to time, returned to Britain subsequently. In the end, as his heirs were all British not living in North America during the revolution, they lost their land inheritances to Virginia confiscations. which appeared to be reversed later by the Supreme

---

[147] ***The Fairfax Grant***
http://www.virginiaplaces.org/settleland/fairfaxgrant.html#two; *Northern Neck Land Proprietary Records* Library of Virginia Compiled by Minor T. Weisiger http://www.lva.virginia.gov/public/guides/rn23_nneckland.pdf;

Court in the case of <u>Fairfax's Devisee v. Hunter's Lessee</u>, but title was confirmed in the commonwealth in <u>Martin v. Hunter's Lessee</u>. [148]

Georgia

Georgia was a crown colony established as a buffer state against the Spanish who then held Florida. Philanthropist first Governor James Edward Oglethorpe and supporters saw it as a haven for the London poor and destitute. It was not considered an economic success until slavery was introduced and limitations on the amount of land ownership were removed..

In the charter to the trustees of Georgia in 1732 , the crown reserved a quit-rent of 4s per 100 acres as a royal revenue and *a* sign of overlordship.' Thus, under the territorial rights conferred by these original charters, a quit-rent was invariably included as the usual sign of a free and common socage tenure, with the crown as the lord of the soil. [149]

In their constitution of 1808, perhaps reflecting the influences of: the imposition of quit-rents; as well as the equalitarian ideals that were promoted when Georgia was first established with its limit on

---

[148] <u>Fairfax's Devisee v. Hunter's Lessee</u>, 11 U.S. (7 Cranch.) 603, 3 L. Ed. 453 (1813), and <u>Martin v. Hunter's Lessee</u> 14 U.S. (1 Wheat.) 304, 4 L. Ed. 97,1816 U.S. LEXIS 333 (1816). http://www.lva.virginia.gov/public/guides/rn23_nneckland.pdf ***Northern Neck Land Proprietary Records*** Library of Virginia, Compiled by Minor T. Weisiger

[149] **Quit-rent System in the American Colonies** by Beverley W. Bond, Jr. Yale University Press (1919) p. 32. For fuller explanation see pp 127-130.

land ownership (50 acres); and original prohibition of slavery (later dropped);[150] and the prohibitions against nobility dating from the time of the Declaration of Independence; the Georgians stated in their constitution that "the property of the soil in a free government" is "one of the essential rights of a free people."[151]

New York

New York came into British possession in 1664 with its own existing Nobility. They were called Patroons (heads of companies). They were granted large tracts of land by the Dutch West Indies Company in the 17th Century with Manorial rights through the Charter of Freedoms and Exemptions of 1629. These manorial rights and privileges were similar to those granted Lords in the Feudal seigneurys. They included the power to establish civil and criminal courts, appoint officials and hold land in perpetuity. At first the tracts were 16 miles long if on one side of the river, or eight miles long if on both sides of the river. In 1640 the size of the tracts were cut in half and any North American Dutch in good standing could buy this noble estate. The Patroons had duties to establish settlements for at least fifty families in four years. Patroonships had their own villages and churches where vital statistics were recorded. Original tenants were granted relief from public taxes for ten years, but were required to pay

---

[150]. http://en.wikipedia.org/wiki/James_Oglethorpe

[151] Thorp 777-802, and especially 794

the Patroons money, goods or services in kind.[152] They were, if effect, little fiefdoms. The tenants, after much controversy, were not fully relieved of their responsibilities until well into the nineteenth century. Of the Dutch it was said:

> "Of peculiar interest were the Dutch landowners of New York, who lived in large and attractive manor houses and ruled their tenants arbitrarily amid elegance and splendor. This landed aristocracy resembled more closely than that of any other colony the landed nobility of Europe. In New York, traders and merchants formed a middle class far below these landowners and not far above the laborers and servants. In New Jersey, Pennsylvania and Delaware, where grants had conflicted and large estates were disrupted, the landed gentry, though still foremost in social rank, were much less elegant in manner and mode of life than those of New York. Here the station of traders and mechanics was consequently improved.."[153]

New York and the Jersies fell into the British hands and the proprietorship of James, Duke of York in 1664 and remained there until he gained the throne in 1685. The Duke's Laws required the reservation of a quit-rent in future land grant patents but, by confirming all Dutch grants under the original terms, the laws

---

[152] http://en.wikipedia.org/wiki/Patroon

[153] **Life in the Early Middle Colonies, New York, New Jersey, Pennsylvania, Delaware, Vermont. A General Historical Survey**
http://www.rootsweb.ancestry.com/~nycoloni/dahistmc.html

permanently waived further feudal dues to the Duke on the lands that

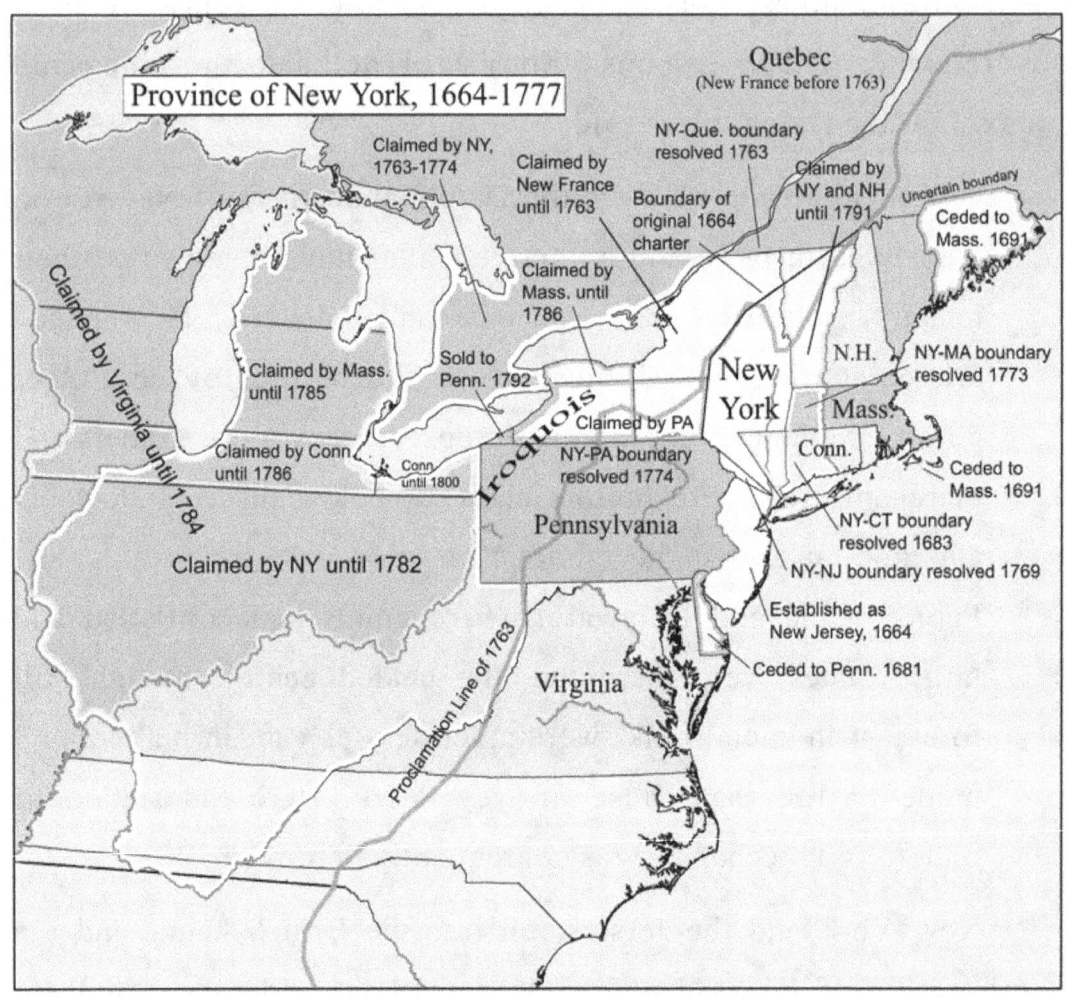

New York with Conflicting Land Claims
http://en.wikipedia.org/wiki/Province_of_New_York/
attributed to Karl Musser, cartographer

were already settled.[154]

This confirmed a number of Dutch manors that included Manor of Rensselaerswyck[155] and Lower Manor at Claverack.[156] Others created after 1664 included the Livingston Manor (Dutchess and Columbia counties) - Robert Livingston the Elder 160,000 acres (650 km²) confirmed by royal charter of George I in 1715, [157] These manors could dwarf many European feudal holdings. Just compare the Churchill estate in the Cotswolds with park of 2,100 acres and the village of Stock presented to the John Churchill, first Duke of Marlborough by Queen Ann from her royal estates for his victory against the French at Blenheim on August 13, 1704.

The decision not to impose quit rents on the Dutch grants prior to 1664 resulted in double standards of land holding and led to discord. There were also problems of omission, lack of specificity and uniformity and lack of enforcement that plagued the collection of quit-rents.[158]

The problems of uniformity were mostly resolved in 1698 when Governor Bellomont received instructions that lands were not to be granted with quit-rents less than two shillings and six pence sterling per hundred acres. This was followed with few exceptions

---

[155] http://en.wikipedia.org/wiki/Manor_of_Rensselaerswyck

[156] http://en.wikipedia.org/wiki/Claverack,_New_York

[157] http://en.wikipedia.org/wiki/Livingston_Manor

[158] Bond, p. 111

until 1774 when new patents were issued for a half penny per acre per year as a fixed amount..[159]

In 1755 a partial correction of the difficulties of collection was passed by the assembly and received the assent of Lieutenant Governor De Lancey.[160] It provided forfeiture without trial and received protest from a prominent member of council and one of the more influential men in New York, William Smith. His protest "reflected the public resentment against any measures that might sanction the claims of the crown to an arbitrary right of enforcement of the quit-rents and the arrears." [161]

> "First, contrary to Magna Carta, the act made it possible to dispossess a man of his freehold by a mere official certificate that a debt was owed, without a verdict of his "equals" or due process of law. Secondly, it deprived debtors to the crown of all pleas and defense. Thirdly, it took away from the subject any common law action or defense when distress was levied for the crown's rents. Finally, said Smith, it "seems contrary to natural justice and equity in that it will subject the lands of a freeholder to sale, tho' the king be indebted to him in a greater sum than is

---

[159] Bond, p. 225

[160] Bond p. 273. Legislative Council Journal, October 30 and November 20, 1754, and ay 28 to July 5, 1755, II, 1168, 1174-1175, 1197-1207; De Lancey to Board of Trade, March 16, 1759, N. Y. Col. Does., VI, 369.

[161] Bond, p. 275

due for quit-rents, and leaves him no remedy either in law or equity in such a case."[162]

Quit-rents were not abolished after independence, but little or no effort was made to collect them on behalf of the state.[163] Perhaps they were considered abolished or forbidden by the bans against feudalism inherent in the absolute prohibitions against granting Titles of Nobility. By then most of the tenants of the large land holders in New York were leaseholders, subject to variable renegotiable rents and so fixed quit-rents were not necessary to maintain the class divisions and could be a distraction from renegotiable rents.

New Jersey

The quit-rent and proprietary situation in the Jerseys is fairly complicated, Before the English, the Dutch had claims, and the area had been partially under the control of the Swedes. From 1638 to 1655 the Swedes had a colony know as New Sweden on both sides of the Delaware River and established a settlement at Fort Nya Elfsborg near Salem, in western New Jersey. In 1655 Peter Stuyvesant seized New Sweden for the Dutch and Dutch West Indies Company. For a time the Swedes and Fins continued to enjoy local antonymy under the Dutch, even having their own militia. The Dutch held it until it was bargained away in a treaty with England in 1664 resolving a war

---

[162] Bond. p. 274, Legislative Council Journal, June 11, 1755, II, 1199. N. Y. Col. MSS., 81, f. 18.

[163] Bond, p. 283-284.

the English had largely lost to the Dutch. The Dutch received some very profitable concessions. During the interim settlers from New England had settled around the Elizabeth- town area, Quakers were settled more in the west and there were in effect, developing two Jersies, East New Jersey, and West New Jersey.

In 1664 Charles II, who had ascended to the English Thrown at the end of the Commonwealth in 1660, granted the property to his brother, James[164] who turned around and granted it to John Lord Berkeley, and Sir George Carteret, on the 24th of June, 1664.[165] The annual rent to James was forty Beaver skins and the annual rent to Berkeley and Carteret was a pepper corn and 20 Nobles per year. Full rights of sub-infatuation were granted in each grant.[166] The name New Jersey appears related to George Carteret (1615 - 1680) a descendent of French ancestry from the Channel island of Jersey. He had held it for Charles I and it was the last Stuart stronghold to surrender to Cromwell, the Lord Protector under the Commonwealth. The name of the Jersey province was also New Caesarea,. John Lord

---

[164] Grant of the Province of Maine : 1664 Charles II to James, Duke of York http://avalon.law.yale.edu/17th_century/me03.asp Thorp...pp. 1637-1640.

[165] **The Duke of York's Release to John Lord Berkeley, and Sir George Carteret, 24th of June, 1664** http://avalon.law.yale.edu/17th_century/nj01.asp, Thorp...pp. 2533-2535.

[166] Sub infeudation is important as in case of escheat, typically death without heirs, the land reverts to the next highest title holder, the higher "lord" or now the "state" in the chain..

Berkeley, and Sir George Carteret we may recall were two of the named proprietors of North and South Carolina in 1663.

In 1764 the Lords proprietors set a quit-rent of half a penny per acre on all new grants of land in the province.[167] In 1680 the Duke of York, for 10 Nobles a year granted West New Jersey to William Penn, Gawn Lawry, Nicholas Lucas, John Eldridge, Edmund Warner, and Edward Byllynge. He granted them his lord proprietorship rights in those lands. These same men were further described by their social rank as Edward Byllynge, gentleman; William Penn, Esq (Squire); Gawn Lawry, merchant; Nicholas Lucas, maulster, John Eldridge, tanner, and Edmond Warner, citizen of London.[168] So the feudal rights of Lords Proprietors could be sold to commoners, a further way recognized in England to create nobility.

Controversy over collection of quit-rents resolved fairly early after 1676 in West New Jersey as they appear to have been abandoned.[169] But the controversy over them continued well into the 18th Century in East Jersey. It came to a head in riots in the middle of

---

[167] **The Concession and Agreement of the Lords Proprietors of the Province of New Caesarea, or New Jersey, to and With All and Every the Adventurers and All Such as Shall Settle or Plant There - 1664** , Thorp....pp. 2535-2544. http://avalon.law.yale.edu/17th_century/nj02.asp

[168] **Duke of York's Second Grant to William Penn, Gawn Lawry, Nicholas Lucas, John Eldridge, Edmund Warner, and Edward Byllynge, for the Soil and Government of West New Jersey-August 6, 1680** , Thorp....pp. 2560-2565. http://avalon.law.yale.edu/17th_century/nj07.asp

[169] Bond, p. 87

the century beginning in 1741 with riots in Newark freeing prisoners who had been detained for trespass for remaining on property forfeit for failure to pay quit rents. Litigation continued to collect the quit-rents and continued to stir the controversies. The opposition:

> " Elizabethtown associates, or the Clinker Lot Men, as they were popularly called,' upheld the validity of their claims and denied the right of the proprietaries of East Jersey to collect quitrents from them."[170]

These positions were considered reminiscent of arguments of Cotton Mather in Massachusetts[171] one phampleter declared:

> "Can any rational man think our predecessors (or indeed any men in their wits) would expose themselves to so great fatigues and costs to bring themselves and their posterity into bondage by being the tributaries of, and to the proprietors"[172]

Bond, publishing in 1919, could observe of this period that:

> The views expressed by one anonymous theorist are decidedly socialistic as regards the ownership of land. "No man," he

---

[170] Bond, p. 102

[171] **The Declaration of the Gentlemen, Merchants, and Inhabitants of Boston, and the Country Adjacent. April 18. 1689**
http://readtheconstitutionstupid.com/en/?option=com_content&view=article&id=2369:1689-boston-declaration-of-grievances-april-18-1689&catid=130&Itemid=744&lang=en; *Origins of Boston's Revolutionary Declaration of 18 April 1689*, Ian K. Steele, *The New England Quarterly*, Vol. 62, No. 1 (Mar., 1989), pp. 75-81

[172] Bond, pp. 104-105

asserts, "is naturally entitled to a greater proportion of the earth than another; but tho' it was made for the equal use of all, it may nevertheless be appropriated by every individual." To prevent the confusion from every man's "being his own carver," governors were appointed by the crown to parcel out the land among its subjects. "But the mischief of it is, that the best parts and most commodiously situated have been granted to a few particulars, in such quantifies that the rest of the subjects have been obliged to buy it for their own use at an extravagant price, a hardship that seems as great as if they - had been put under the necessity of buying the waters of the rivers."[173]

Clearly the arguments were against unequal power and disparity of wealth portrayed by the nobility and this was a constant, recurring theme well before the English-American Revolution of 1775. While the proprietors maintain the right to quit-rents up to the revolution, there appears little attempt to collect after 1752.[174]

Main

Main was first granted to the proprietors, Sir Ferdinando George and John Mason, Esq. and others as "one Body Politique and Corporate perpetuall" in August, 1622 by James I naming them as "President and Councill established at Plymouth in the county of

---

[173] Bond, p. 105

[174] Bond, ibid

Devon, for the planting, ruling and governing of New-England in America."[175] The grant included "all prerogatives, jurisdictions, royaltys, privileges, franchises and preliminaries within any of the said territories and precincts thereof whatsoever." It was regranted to the proprietor, Sir Ferdinando George in 1639. by Charles ! with full palatine rights.[176] In 1664 Charles II granted the province to his brother, James, Duke of York, without the Palatine powers but with powers equally as large expressly stated.[177] Broader grants were extended to James by his brother in 1674.[178]

The English, like the Dutch in New Netherlands, could and did at times grant sub-infatuation rights to corporations. It is clear that the powers at the time were intermingled feudal and more modern mercantile economic concepts of possession power and the exercise of power, and had already been figured out in the rankings to be found within the exercise of possession and power. Looking at New York, the actual traditional feudal names can be seen as far less important than holding the legally protected rights of power.

New Hampshire

New Hampshire was part of he Province of New England granted to the Duke of York. It was subject to a number of grants:

---

[175] Thorp, 1621-1625

[176] Thorp, 1625-1637

[177] Thorp, 1637-1640

[178] Thorp, 1641-1644

1629 - Grant of Hampshire to Capt. John Mason, 7th of November; 1629[179] - Grant of Laconia to Sir Ferdinando Gorges and Captain John Mason by the Council for New England; November 17; 1635[180] - Grant of the Province of New Hampshire to John Wollaston, Esq.; 1635[181] - Grant of the Province of New Hampshire From Mr. Wollaston to Mr. Mason, 11th June; 1635 - Grant of the Province of New Hampshire to Mr. Mason, 22 April,[182]   By the Name of Masonia; 1635 - Grant of the Province of New Hampshire to Mr. Mason, 22 Apr., By the Name of New Hampshire; and 1635 - Grant of His Interest in New Hampshire by Sir Ferdinando Gorges to Captain John Mason; September 17.[183]

The original charter granted the incorporated proprietor "all perogatives jurisdictions, royalties, privileges, franchises, and preheminences within any of the said territories and precincts thereof whatsoever...."[184] This was quite enough in 1629 to make the perpetual corporation the feudal lord. However those from New Hampshire chose to live more in the New England way of governing themselves, as seen in the Agreement of the Settlers at Exeter in

---

[179] Thorp, pp. 2433-2466

[180] Thorp pp. 2441-2443

[181] Thorp pp. 2437-2440

[182] Thorp pp. 2443-2444

[183] http://avalon.law.yale.edu/subject_menus/statech.asp#nh

[184] http://avalon.law.yale.edu/17th_century/charter_003.asp, Thorp..pp. 2433-2434.

New Hampshire, 1639,[185] and The Combinations of the Inhabitants Upon the Piscataqua River for Government, 1641.[186]

Connecticut

Connecticut was unique in having formed itself into government that continued through the Commonwealth, and was successful in petitioning Charles II for its own corporate charter in 1662. This charter named the original corporate incorporators and.

"all such others as now are, or hereafter shall be admitted and made free of the Company and Society of Our Colony of Connecticut, in America, shall from Time to Time, and for ever hereafter, be One Body Corporate and politique, in Fact and Name, by the Name of, Governor and Company of the English colony of Connecticut in New-England, in America;...."[187]

Edmond Andros tried to take the charter, but it was famously hidden in an oak tree. Thus Connecticut never had the seal of nobility place on its lands.

Pennsylvania

Pennsylvania was granted to William Penn by Charter from Charles II on February 28, 1681 as "a province and Segniory and

---

[185] http://avalon.law.yale.edu/17th_century/nh06.asp Thorp p 2445

[186] http://avalon.law.yale.edu/17th_century/nh07.asp Thorp p. 2445

[187] http://avalon.law.yale.edu/17th_century/ct03.asp Thorp pp. 529-536

doe call it Pennsilvania"...."in Free and common Soccage, by fealty only for all Services and not in Capite or by Knights Service," for two beaver skins and one fifth of the gold and silver discovered, per year, and for cancellation of a £16,000 debt owed by the monarch to Penn's father Admiral William Penn, who had supported Charles and the Stuarts during the Commonwealth. So William Penn started out as the Lord Proprietor over the province of Pennsylvania with all the right inherent in a Segniory of the crown, to set up government, establish courts, sell land on such terms as he pleased reserving only the final rights of the crown in case of escheat or forfeiture. Although never mentioned in the Charter, "Penn's right to reserve quit-rents was never questioned."[188, 189]

---

[188] Bond, p. 31.

[189] **The following table shows the annual value and the variations in the quit-rents in 1776:**

12,000 acres @ one beaver skin per 12,000 acres £	0 6s 0	
45,951 acres @ two beaver skins per 60,000 acres	9s 2%d	
856,895% acres @ is per 100 acres	428 8s 11 d	
176,760 acres @ is per 1,000 acres	8 16s 9 d	
1,385,219% acres @ d per acre	2,885 17s 5%d	
1,629,279 acres @ ld per acre	6,788 13s 3 d	
37,037¹ acres @ 1 bushel of wheat per 100 acres	55 lls	
4,571% acres @ 4s per 100 acres	9 2s 10%d	
46,511% acres @ various rents	26 15s 2 d	
100,000 acres @ an Indian corn		
40,000 acres @ a Red Rose per 10,000 acres		
4,334,226 acres £10,204	7%d	

[% could be ¼ ½ or ¾ pence. Probably poor Google reproduction]

Bond, p. 134, n. 3.

William Penn modified rights from the original charter[190] in his various public decrees: July 11, 1681 - Concessions to the Province of Pennsylvania[191]; April 25, 1682 - Charter of Liberties;[192] May 5, 1682 - Frame of Government of Pennsylvania; February 2 1682[193] - Frame of government of 1683;[194] Frame of Government of Pennsylvania; 1696;[195] Charter of Privileges Granted by William Penn, Esq. to the Inhabitants of Pennsylvania and Territories, October 28, 1701.[196]

"Practically no exemptions from the quit-rents were allowed, and even Penn's children paid some form of acknowledgment yearly for their private estates.' This strict rule was broken once only, in 1755, when, in order to promote settlement on the frontier, grants were authorized in this region with a quit-rent of either a halfpenny or a farthing per acre, but with an exemption from payment until 1786."[197]

---

[190] Thorp pp. 3035-3044

[191] Thorp pp. 3044-3047

[192] Thorp pp. 3047-3052

[193] Thorp pp. 3052-3063

[194] Thorp pp. 3064-3069

[195] Thorp pp. 3070-3076

[196] Thorp pp. 3076-3081

[197] Bond, p. 136.

Opposition to quit-rents began to show in 1701 when the assembly offered to buy them out, an offer refused by Penn. The opposition grew with the development of proprietary and anti-proprietary parties.[198] The argument over ultimate control over quit-rents and whether proprietary properties were exempt from legislative authority continued for over a half century as the governor, on instructions from the proprietors, continued to veto bills to tax or control the proprietor's property. In 1755, responding to a critical need to support troops on the Pennsylvania frontier against the French and Indians, Thomas Penn made a gift of £5,000 out of quit rent receipts in lieu of being taxed provided the legislature abandoned its demand to tax the proprietor's property. It did, but in the following years, the Penns did not make that concession. Finally, with unpaid troops on the frontier and the legislature refusing to raise any more money to support them unless the governor allowed bills to tax the Proprietor's property, by raising a £100,000 with a tax on all property, "the estates of the proprietors not excepted."[199] in 1757 when the troops had not been paid in six months and half were refusing to march the quest and the whole lost rather than these instructions be departed from" Governor Denny dilemma was raised and faced. With the question: "Must the country be destroyed he relented and the tax was passed. The same

---

[198] Bond, p. 138.

[199] Bond, p. 153 (Consider today what it would costs to keep a contingent of an army in the field and one begins to understand the cost and value comparisons)

necessity arose again in 1759 with the same result. These acts constituted a successful denial of the Proprietor's "absolute feudal rights in Pennsylvania."[200]

But the controversy continued with threats of disallowance of taxing proprietors rights subject to actions of the Privy Council in London, and problems of identifying and collecting the taxes in Pennsylvania further exacerbated by the fact that the quite-rents were payable in local currency while the tax was due in sterling. The controversies continued until the Revolution when the quit-rents came under the scrutiny of the new government

Chief Justice McKean, in an opinion he delivered to a committee of the assembly, denied that these charges had been reserved for the support of the government. Just as in other American proprieties, he held, the quit-rents of Pennsylvania originated under the rights of the mesne lord, William Penn, and were, therefore, feudal dues at the absolute disposal of the proprietary.' After the receipt of this opinion, the committee reported that the feudal rights of Penn's heirs should not be allowed,[201] and in

---

[200] Bond, p. 154, generally pp. 137-164

[201] Bond, p. 160: "The report of the committee asserted that the quit-rents were utterly subservient of the rights, safety, and happiness of the good people of this state and dangerous to civil liberty in general, as evidently tending to revive and confirm an unwarrantable aristocratical power and influence within this state, inconsistent with its true interests and therefore not to be admitted in a government founded upon equal liberty and the authority of the people.'" Cadwalader, Richard McCall, **A Practical Treatise on Law of Ground Rents in Pennsylvania**, , pp. 46-47.

the divesting act the assembly clearly distinguished between these rights and the private property of the proprietaries. The former, represented by the quit-rents and the purchase money, they summarily abolished, at the same time relieving all lands of any arrears, but the latter, including the reserved manors and the manorial rents, they confirmed. With a sense of justice that was unique at this time, the assembly compensated the Penn family for the loss of their proprietary rights by a gift of £130,000 "in remembrance of the enterprising spirit of the founder, and of the expectations and dependence of his successors."[202]

It is estimated that in 1779 there was uncollected and owing to the Penn Proprietors quit rents amounting to £118,569 4s 61 ½d. [203]

Delaware

In addition to county taxes, colonial Delaware landowners had to pay annual quit-rents to the proprietor.[204] But it was a complicated and contentious system aggravated by the variety and inconsistency of applications owing not only to the Penns but also to the prior proprietors and settlers.

---

[202] Bond, p. 160

[203] Ibid. P. 162

[204] http://www.ancestry.com/wiki/index.php?title=Delaware_Land_Records

Atlantic Colonial Aristocracy

There were further reasons to fear nobility in America, as Benjamin Rush, one of the founders had in 1777 observed, was that disparities in wealth and power in America had already sowed the seeds for the creation of nobility in America.[205] This confirms the historical observations of William Cecil Headrick who observed in 1941 that during the one hundred and fifty years leading up to the revolution two distinct classes of colonists had developed, socially and economically. He included the "well born" group of land owners (some of whom we see were certainly very well born, togther with merchants and money lenders.[206]

Harvard College students' names, to the eve of the Revolution, were arranged in the order of the respectability of their parentage. John Hancock could be considered an example of the first, raised by his uncle Thomas Hancock, perhaps the richest merchant in New England, educated at Harvard, sent to England by his uncle for further understanding, inherited his uncles business and fleet of trading ships. He was one of the richest men in America even owning about 1,000 acres of land in New England, which was a

---

[205] Benjamin Rush, **Observations upon the Present Government of Pennsylvania** 8 (Phila., Styner & Cist 1777).

[206] *A Study of Social Stratification With Reference to Social Class Barriers and Social Class Rigidity* by William Cecil Headrick. (Excerpt from Chapter 11 Social Class Rigidities In Colonial America) Submitted in partial fulfillment of the requirements for the degree of Doctor of Philosophy at New York State University. December 1, 1941.

large holding in New England. Another was the industrialist lawyer, Daniel Leonard, who remained a loyalist and whose family made their fortune from ironworks in New England. He wrote under the name of "Massachusettensis" in opposition to John Adams' "Novanglus." His property, like that of some other loyalists, was confiscated. Some, like William Allen of Pennsylvania who was a successful merchant and land speculator, kept quiet during the revolution though opposing it before hand. While Hancock could hardly be considered a conservative, the Allens and Leonards and many others of the rich could be included in the loyalists who perhaps numbered in 15 to 20 percent of the Atlantic colonialists at the time.

There was a constant need for specie in dealing with import trade from England as English were prohibited from exporting their own currency so none would be available in north America and had to be supplied from elsewhere. Smaller traders who had built up no great account balances in England came to depend on the money lenders who could provide them with "Sterling bills of Exchange." Such a rich money lender was Haym Solomon, a Polish Jew emigree moving to New York in 1770, who, like Hancock, used his wealth in support of the revolution. He arranged the financing of Washington's army's participation in the Yorktown campaign that ended the war. So, while Headrick may have been accurate in describing a class society, it should not be implied that class divisions always determined who was on what side of the revolution. Still, to raise an effective army, perhaps the appeal to class distinctions was a benefit to the leaders of the revolutionaries? But should the constitutional principles in the nobility restrictions be reduced to a propaganda or recruitment ploy?

Headrick appears to be accurate when he said as a general principal that the "rich and the well-born -- of merchants, large landholders, and money-lenders -- dominated every phase of colonial life."[207] Some may have appeared snobbish, as he reports, but some, such as Hancock, certainly did not or he would never have kept his popularity, even if he was a known fashion manakin. In any event, we support Headrick's general proposition that: "The early classes of the colonies were counterparts of the European social classes -- except for an overabundance of middle class elements in New England and eastern Pennsylvania,...."[208] He insists there was much social immobility as we entered the revolution, and much stratification and social rigidity.

For example many of the leading colonial gentlemen possessed armorial rights such as the Washingtons, Harrisons, Balls, Berkeleys, Byrds, Pages, Carys, Bollings, Clairbornes, Burwells, and others in Virginia," and "the Penns, Logans, Penningtons, Lloyds and numerous Pennsylvania families," and others in New

---

[207] Hedrick, supra.

[208] Ibid.

107

Jersey, Delaware, New York, New England and Southern Colonies.[209]

George Washington's life allows us to examine colonial, and especially Virginia aristocracy. He was born into middling aristocracy as the first son of the slave owning Virginia planter Augustine Washington (1694–1743) and his second wife, Mary Ball Washington (1708–1789). His birth was in February 11, 1731 of the old calendar and February 22, 1732 under the new calendar adopted in 1750. The Washingtons were part of the moderately prosperous gentry in Virginia. George had two older half-brothers, Lawrence and Augustine, from his father's first marriage to Jane Butler Washington. His father died when he was eleven putting him under the tutelage of his oldest half brother, Lawrence with further mentoring from William Fairfax, who was Lawrence's father-in-law and cousin of Virginia's largest landowner, Thomas, Lord Fairfax, who gave George his first job as a surveyor.[210]

George's older brothers had been educated in England at the Appleby School, but the death of his father at the age of eleven prevented George from following in their footsteps. He received tutoring and some schooling in Fredericksburg. at an Anglican school. The Lawrence connection to the Fairfax family enabled George to obtain an appointment at age 17 in 1749, as the official

---

[209] Ibid

[210] http://en.wikipedia.org/wiki/George_Washington

surveyor for Culpeper County. This well-paid position provided him opportunities to purchase land in the Shenandoah Valley, leading to further acquisitions in Western Virginia. George's brothers Lawrence and Augustine, Jr. participated in the Ohio Company, a land investment company granted 500,000 acres in the Ohio Valley between the Kanawha River and Monongahela in 1649 by King George II. They were joined by other Virginia investors. Lawrence's his rank as commander of the Virginia militia, brought his younger brother George to the attention of new governor to be of Virginia, Robert Dinwiddie. Dinwiddie became an investor in the Ohio Company and supporter of George and when Lawrence died, George became one of four to succeed him in the militia ranks. Young George, at the age of 22, leading a Virginia expedition to war to persuade the French to leave the Ohio Territory, ambushed the French in the Battle of Jumonville Glen in May 1754, thus beginning the hostilities of the French and Indian War, also known as the Seven Years War. Later this led to George becoming second in command of the British Western expedition against the French in the Ohio area.. He assumed command of the defeated army after General Edward Braddock was mortally wounded in the Battle of the Monongahela. Daniel Boone was one of the wagon masters in that expedition..[211]   That war interrupted the Ohio Company's

---

[211] Ibid, http://en.wikipedia.org/wiki/French_and_Indian_War, http://en.wikipedia.org/wiki/Edward_Braddock, http://en.wikipedia.org/wiki/Daniel_Boone

(and the Washington investment) development. Renewal of the grants were interrupted by Pontiac's War and George III 1763 proclamation line describing the western territory as Indian reserve that could now only be purchased from the native Americans by the crown. No longer could the colony of Virginia or the Ohio Company rely on a friendship treaty with local tribes in made 1752 at the native village of Logstown[212] in what is now western Pennsylvania or expect to recoup its expenses for the work of Christopher Gist to explore the Ohio Valley in order to identify lands for potential settlement. These could be written off as possibly all lost. He had begun his surveys in 1750-1753, estimating the Kanawhan Region and Ohio Valley tributaries.[213] So a war, and a Native uprising together with the change of a king to George III in 1760, destroyed the investments of the Ohio company to 1763 when it wanted to renew its grants.

On January 6, 1759, George Washington married the wealthy widow Martha Dandridge Custis. They raised two of her children and later two of her grand children. George had none of his own. His marriage and his inheritances from his father, Augustine Sr. and his brother Lawrence, made him one of Virginia's richest men and certainly increased his social standing. He had inherited landed

---

[212] (1725?, 1727–1758, also Logg's Town, French: *Chiningue* pronounced Shenango)

[213] http://en.wikipedia.org/wiki/Ohio_Company

wealth and chattels (personal property) including slaves from his father, Augustine Sr. and his brother Lawrence. He enjoyed an aristocratic lifestyle with fox hunting, going to dances and parties, in addition to the theater, races, and cockfights. Washington played cards and backgammon, and played billiards. He followed the common aristocratic practice of importing luxuries and other goods from England and paying for them with his tobacco exports.[214] He really typifies the colonial aristocracy described by Headrick.

Headrick summed up the requirements for membership and advancement in the Atlantic Colonies had been largely tied up by 1700.:

> "In all the colonies, the councils were almost wholly made up of the members of these small aristocracies, or plutocracies, and as the suffrage was very limited, their influence extended to the assemblies . . . the aristocrats by 1700 were fastening a firm grip both on the political management and commercial exploitation of the New World.."[215]

---

[214] Ibid

[215] Headrick, supra.

111

CHAPTER IV

RELATED CANADIAN NOBILITY AND EUROPEAN BACKGROUND

In 1619 James I erected the Baronetage of Ireland and laid plans for a further new Baronetage with the object of assisting the colonization of Nova Scotia. However in 1624 he died before this could be implemented. In 1625 Charles I took up the previous plans and erected the Baronetage of Scotland and Nova Scotia.(new Scotland). The new baronets were each required to pay 2,000 marks or enough to support six settlers for two years. Over a hundred of these baronetcies, now known as Scottish baronetcies, have survived to this day.[216]

Sir Thomas Temple was created a Nova Scotia baronet by Charles II on July7, 1662 . He sided with Parliament against the king and Cromwell granted him a proprietorship in Main and Nova Scotia, the area of Arcadia. He established his headquarters at Penobscot (now Castine, Main) with forts at Port Royal and St. John. His property rights proved to be at the whim of diplomacy of greater lords. In the Treaty of Breda of 1667. Arcadia, without clearly establishing its boundaries, was awarded to France. Temple, who was then residing in Boston, saw his Cromwellian charter never recognized and in 1670 finally turned his proprietorship over to France. He moved to London where he died in1674. He was an

---

[216] http://en.wikipedia.org/wiki/Baronet

early English nobleman, lord proprietor, living for some time in North America, and proprietor of property ultimately both in the United States and Canada..[217]

The Seignuerial System was introduced into Canada (New France) in the early seventeenth Century by the French crown as the primary means to encourage settlement. It was generally attributed to Cardinal Richelieu's actions in1627, but it was hardly a new idea at the time. The Spanish had experienced a similar system in helping to resettle lands in Charlemagne's time. The Germans had used it to populate lands to the east to take the places of Slavs either killed or driven out.

The title of Seigneur was a title of nobility both in England and France. Authority for this can be found in the work of John Selden (1584 - 1654), English Jurist, scholar and antiquarian. He provides several examples: William Earl of Salisbury styled himself as Lord of Man or Seignor de Man.;[218]   The Earl of Salisbury's stile in it is Gilliam Conte de Sarisbiry, Seignior de Man & de V Isle de Wight.[219]   Selden cites another Englishman "Counts d' Arundel Seigneurs del Chattel, honour &Seigneurie d' Arundel

---

[217] http://en.wikipedia.org/wiki/Temple_Baronets, http://en.wikipedia.org/wiki/Thomas_Temple.

[218] John Selden, Titles of Honour (1672) p. 25.

[219] Ibid.

ount ewe lour lieu a (ten t & feilx, time out of mind."[220]   The French used the terms "Seigniory of the Daulphin" and "Seigniors du fang" possibly tracing back before "the Ages ...the Carolin Line began."(732-843ce).[221]

The Castilian nobility in the Golden Age included powerful grandees and other fabulously wealthy titled aristocrats, to lesser nobles down to the Cervantes' Don Quixote and even poorer hidalgos who had to perform manual labor to keep from starving, reflecting the enormous disparities in the scale of property ownership and land control.[222]

> "[B]y the reign of Charles V (1516-1558) privileges of nobility were openly sold to whoever could pay for them, as a means of increasing royal revenues. Hidalguía (noble status) was desirable because it conferred not only social prestige, but also immunity from direct royal taxation, and certain legal privileges as well."[223]

What were those privileges?

---

[220] Ibid 730-731.

[221] Ibid p 399-401

[222] **Land and Society in Golden Age Castile**,(Cambridge Iberian and Latin American Studies) David E. Vassberg, Cambridge University Press (1984) p. 91 .http://libro.uca.edu/vassberg/land4.htm,

[223] Ibid.

The privileges of a hidalgo were fairly clearly delineated. Hidalgos were less threatened than others by the law and were distinguished from the rest of society. A hidalgo had a special relationship with the king and could only be arrested by his express order. Out of respect for his military calling, a hidalgo's horses and weapons were exempt from seizure for debt or any other cause and because of his supposed virtue and purity of blood he might not be judicially tortured. Affairs of honour between nobles were settled by duel and if a noble had for some reason to suffer the death penalty, he was beheaded and not hanged. These privileges naturally applied to the titled nobility as well. [224]

Consequentially it is as improper to consider the Hidalguía of Spain as one economic, political or social status as it is to consider the corporation and corporatism as one form of economic representation, society or power today. All have been for sale to be purchased from the Monarch or the State and the later is far more common than even those nobles like Miguel de Cervantes' hero, the Hidalgo Don Quixote, of the past. Today we have corporations covering from General Electric and Wells Fargo to your local physician or plumber. Until the fourteenth century in Spain, the rich hidalgos were frequently distinguished from the rest of the hidalgos

---

[224] John Edwards: **Christian Córdoba: The city and its region in the late Middle Ages**, Chapter 5 *The nobility in regional politics*, p. 132, http://alfredjordanpacheco.com/ajp19.htm

by the title of "*rico hombre*" (rich man). That really simplifies our definitions of all great nobility in the west. If we use the legal word person, that includes rich corporations. So there is another title of nobility to add to our list. Until the late middle ages saw the introduction of the French titles such as "duke, marquis, count and viscount were introduced" this was the only title of distinction for "the leading magnates of Castile." and only "begun to appear among the Córdoba aristocracy by 1500." [225]

The English have a history of relying on rich men to be the advisers of government before their aristocracy ossified through inheritance. In the later thirteenth and early fourteenth century, during a period when barony was abandoned as the basis of the issuance of summons, men were called to council the King in government, to be in what came to be known as Parliament, by reason of their power and wealth.[226] We could say that the power and wealth proceeded the formal title of recognition lay at their foundation and was the true basis for their distinctions at least until more modern times when merit was commonly recognized in life peerages.

Settlement by creation of manors dates back to at least to 778 CE and Charlemagne's efforts to resettle Visigothic refugees in the

---

[225] Ibid,

[226] Sidney Painter, **Studies In The History of the English Feudal Barony**, pp. 56, 176, 197. The Johns Hopkins University Studies In Historical and Social Science Series LXI Number 3, 1943.

south of France who had joined with his Forces after his withdrawal from the disappointing siege of Zaragoz, the biggest Muslim controlled city in Northern Spain.[227]   He settled them on manors consisting of the demesne for the lord and his family; the dependents' (serfs' or villeins') holdings; and the free peasants' land. This is practically the same formula used to settle Quebec by the French. Lords were also given certain rights for services and/or payment by the tenants and control over local justice and had duties to provide for protection.   Feudalism was also introduced into Aragon and Catalonia from France during the reconquista.[228]

More attractive manorial tenantry promoted by German princes during the reigns of the Hohenstaufen (1138-1254). This was led by the Germans following Teutonic Knights to expand into the conquered areas of Slavic lands in the east including Pomerania, Silesia, Bohemia, and Moravia.[229] . The land at the time and until into the 19th century in Europe and North America, remained the primary means of production, whether from agriculture or extraction or both. Here we see the rich and powerful leading the way and doing so by furnishing subsistence to some those of lesser fortune as

---

[227] http://en.wikipedia.org/wiki/Manorialism,

http://en.wikipedia.org/wiki/Battle_of_Roncevaux_Pass_(778)

[228] http://www.mongabay.com/reference/country_studies/spain/HISTORY.html

[229] Medieval Germany -- The Empire Under the Early Habsburgs
http://www.germanculture.com.ua/library/history/bl_habsburgs.htm

tenants, villeins or serfs. This is somewhat similar to private enterprise providing income, except the serfs and villeins and even free peasants generally got more in the form of homes protection and a subsistence type of agriculture for food and clothing.. Nobility did not exist solely for profit.

Canadian Seigneurial System

The dominant pre-evolutionary form of land distribution in Canada was the Seignuerial system was established in New France in 1627. It survived the victory and conquest by the British in 1763 in the French and Indian War (Seven Year War), not to be officially abolished until 1854.[230] It follows typical French settlement policies since the middle ages inspired by the feudal system of establishing manors with of lords (seignors) occupying land and censitaires, normally referred to as habitants paying certain dues for the right to live on and work those parcels on those manors.

The Compagnie des cent associés, was granted ownership and legal and Seignuerial rights over New France and it performed the sub-infeudation in the form of manorial tenancies. So both the English and the French introduced and supported a class system with nobility into North America from the very early seventeenth century. The French granted fiefs to the influential colonists who could

---

[230] For more on the general descriptions that follow see **Seignuerial System of New France** http://en.wikipedia.org/wiki/Seigneurial_system_of_New_France; **Seignuerial System** http://thecanadianencyclopedia.com/en/article/Seignuerial-system/

118

promise immigration and support a manor including a mill for the grain to be raised for local sustenance and as a point of defense. They could then divide the land, retain a part and settling the tenants (habitants or censitaires) on sections of the rest in regular plots with access to the waterways for transportation.

The Seigneuries (Manors) were generally promoted in a systematic way, rectangular grants approximately 5 x 15 kilometers in size, and divided, where possible, into river lots, following a system utilized in Normandy. This produced long, .rectangular plots encouraging neighbor interaction and providing points of access to the common means of travel, the rivers. The individual plots were large enough to provide a subsistence living with some possible profit. The system provided a well defined relationship between the habitants and seigneurs. Usually leases between the seigneurs and habitants were based on notarized contracts that described the rights and obligations of each party.

The seigneur could establish a law courts, had to operate a mill and could organize a commune (townships or incorporated

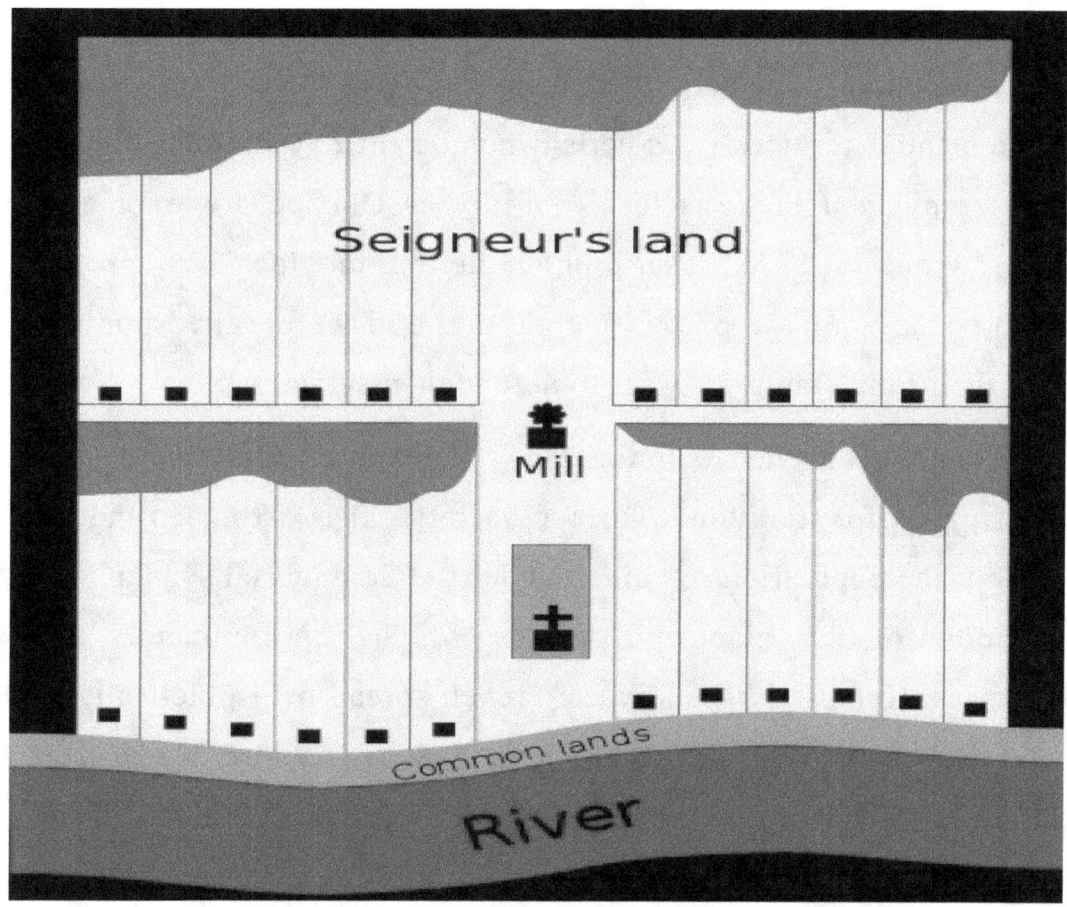

Typical Seigneury Tenant allotments for 24 tenants
http://en.wikipedia.org/wiki/Seigneurial_system_of_New_France
GNU Free Documentation License

municipalities in the United States or *Gemeinden* in Germany). He received a variety of forms of rent: the cens,[231] a small feudal ancient

---

[231] The cens' was a nominal tax or land tax that replaced the *taille'*, a direct tax levied on individuals in France. In New France settlers were also called

tithe; reaffirming the habitant's subjection to the seigneur; the *rente* (rent) in cash or kind; and banalités of taxes levied on grain that the habitant was required to grind in his seigneur's mill. The seigneur also frequently granted hunting, fishing and cutting licences. In the early 18th century, seigneurs began to require that their habitants to provide manual services for a certain number of days annually. The British recognized them as local nobility as Quebec governor Guy Carlton wrote in 1775 describing gathering the locals to protect Canada "The Noblesse of this Neighbourhood were called upon to collect their Inhabitants, in order to defend themselves...."[232]

Central to French colonization, the Seignuerial system was a major support for traditional Québec society. It is estimated that 75 to 80% of the population remained under the Seignuerial system until the middle of the nineteenth century. The approximately 200 seigneuries were established by the French spread over practically all inhabited areas along both banks of the St. Lawrence River from Montreal to Québec as well as in the Richelieu and Chaudière valleys and extending on to the Gaspé. Those holding seigneuries included nobility, religious institutions, military officers and government administrators. So there was a sizable group of nobility in Canada

censitaires', derived from this word that also relates to the word "census.' The register in which the seigneur wrote the date and the amount paid each year by the censitaires was known as the *censier.'* http://richardjohnbr.blogspot.com/2010/10/Seignuerial-system-and-settlement.html

[232] http://en.wikipedia.org/wiki/Quebec_Act

when the British took over in 1763. And the British confirmed and extended it.

More recent reevaluation of the Seignuerial system has observed:

> "The Seignuerial system is often presented as a basic form of land distribution and occupation. However, recent studies have called for a re-evaluation of this traditional interpretation and have highlighted an aspect of the Seignuerial system that is often neglected. As an institution, the Seignuerial system played a leading role in building and maintaining social relations in New France. According to some historians, it represents [translation] "the essence of the social hierarchy and inequality that characterized pre-revolutionary France." Whether they were of noble or common descent, the seigneurs were a privileged class, and their relationships with the censitaires were affected by the perception of the cens. However, this is not to suggest that the seigneur oppressed the censitaire. The availability of land in the 17th and 18th centuries allowed habitants to choose where to settle. Furthermore, seigneurs who were too demanding, who were absentee landowners, or who neglected to develop their lands were less likely to attract settlers."[233]

---

[233] Seignuerial System in Canada
http://thecanadianencyclopedia.com/en/article/Seignuerial-system/
"Censitaires (habitants) who were unable to pay back the capital of their

rentes would be obliged to make annual royalty payments called *rentes constituées*, which were payable in perpetuity. Every year on St. Martin's Day (11 November), censitaires would present themselves at the seigneurial manor to pay their rentes. While the *Seigniorial Act* of 1854 abolished the system of rights and obligations, neither Seignuerial property nor the relationship between seigneur and censitaire was abolished. In 1928, an inquiry launched by the Bureau de la statistique du Québec (Statistics Québec) showed that rentes were still being collected in 190 seigneuries (for a total capital value of $3,577,573). The annual payments made by nearly 60,000 families amounted to more than $200,000.

"In 1935, the Québec government created the Syndicat national, or SNRRS (National Commission for the Repurchase of Seignuerial Rentes), in an effort to put an end to the Seignuerial system once and for all. Its mandate was to make, on behalf of independent cities and towns and county councils, the final payments of rentes constituées to those who held Seignuerial rights over their land. To achieve this, the SNRRS took out a government-secured loan and became the creditor for several municipalities in Québec. In exchange, these municipalities were required to create a special tax roll that would establish the amount of each censitaire's annual payment to the SNRRS in addition to property taxes. The amount received was then transferred to the SNRRS to be used to repay the loan over a 41-year period. The last payment made by the municipalities to the SNRRS was in 1970. Some censitaires paid this municipal "tax," established to replace the former system of the rente constituée, over a period of 30 years.

"In short, the impact and importance of the Seignuerial system goes beyond landscape and toponymy (see place names). It left an important mark on the history of some municipalities in Québec. Some former seigneurs played central roles in municipal politics and became the first mayors of their localities. Furthermore, some Seignuerial families continue to be remembered in Québec. For example, in the 20th century, several Seignuerial honours were bestowed on descendants of Seignuerial families, including Pierre Boucher of Boucherville. who was interred beneath the Sainte-Famille church in Boucherville in 1957. Perceptions of the Tessier family of Beauport and the Taschereau family of SainteMarie de Beauce are influenced by their ties to the Seignuerial system."

The British Takeover in 1763

With the defeat of the French and the ceding of the French claims in North America in the 1763 Treaty of Paris, many of the colonists could have reasonable expectations that the Colonial land claims between the Appalachian Mountains and the Mississippi River could be realized. This should have opened up the Ohio and Illinois territories and all or parts of the future states west of the Appalachians of Alabama, Mississippi, Tennessee, Kentucky, Indiana, Ohio, Illinois, Michigan, Minnesota, Wisconsin, western New York, Western Pennsylvania, all of present West Virginia except the Eastern Panhandle. and parts of Acadia; Quebec and upper French Canada, over 625,000 square miles (over one million square kilometers) in State territory alone.

It is estimated that the area of land cut off by George III's 1763 line from future development by Atlantic Colonial claims would be 236,825,600 acres (958,399 km²), or 10.4 percent of current United States territory, and make up all or part of 10 states.[234]. Seven of the colonies, largely based upon the vagueness of the boundaries in the original colonial charter land descriptions, had western land claims in

---

[234] http://en.wikipedia.org/wiki/State_cessions

these areas.[235] The prior New England crown land grab of James II of the 1680's pails in comparison.

The commonwealth of **Virginia** asserted its right to a tract that fanned out to the west and north, encompassing the expanses of the Old Northwest (the Ohio country).

Virginia surrendered its claim to the Northwest in 1784, only holding on to the rich lands directly across the mountains until the new federal government was in place. Those lands became Kentucky in 1792 when Virginia formally vacated its claim.

Connecticut put forth a claim to a strip of land from its western boundary to the Mississippi River. It also made a claim to a portion of Pennsylvania.. Connecticut and New York jointly claimed lands in the Old Northwest. New York surrendered its rights in 1785 and Connecticut followed the next year. However, Connecticut's claim to an area known as the Western Reserve was maintained until 1795, when it was purchased by the Connecticut Land Company.

Massachusetts made claim to a portion of present-day Michigan and Wisconsin. This was surrendered by Massachusetts in 1785 together with a much weaker claim to an area in western New York that was given up in 1786. East of the Appalachians,

---

[235] United State History: Western Land Claims
http://www.u-s-history.com/pages/h1160.htm The following comments are a synopsis of the claims of seen colonies to the lands generally between the Alleghenies and the Mississippi taken from this site.

Massachusetts vied with New Hampshire and New York to claim Vermont, which achieved statehood in 1791.

In 1782, **New York** ceded its claim to a large tract that included much of present-day Ohio, Indiana, Illinois, Michigan, Kentucky and portions of central Tennessee and western Virginia.

North Carolina attempted to surrender its western claims in 1784, probably because of the expense in maintaining those claims.. Settlers in what would later become Tennessee, particularly along the Watauga River, paid few taxes, but demanded assistance with fending off Indian attacks. It was not until 1790 that the central government accepted North Carolina's cession.

In 1787, **South Carolina** gave up its claim to a narrow strip of land running from its western boundary to the Mississippi River. Part of this claim was added to northern Georgia and the remainder was ceded to the central government.

Georgia possessed perhaps the weakest claim to western lands, and held out the longest. The area that later became Alabama and Mississippi were given up in 1802.

So George III's land grab in 1763, later confirmed by Parliament in 1774 must have provided a sever shock to the land speculators of the Colonies, striping them of many existing and potential land claims to fertile areas larger again than the thirteen colonies. Washington, as one of these western land speculators, had much more to be disappointed from the English actions than their failure to grant

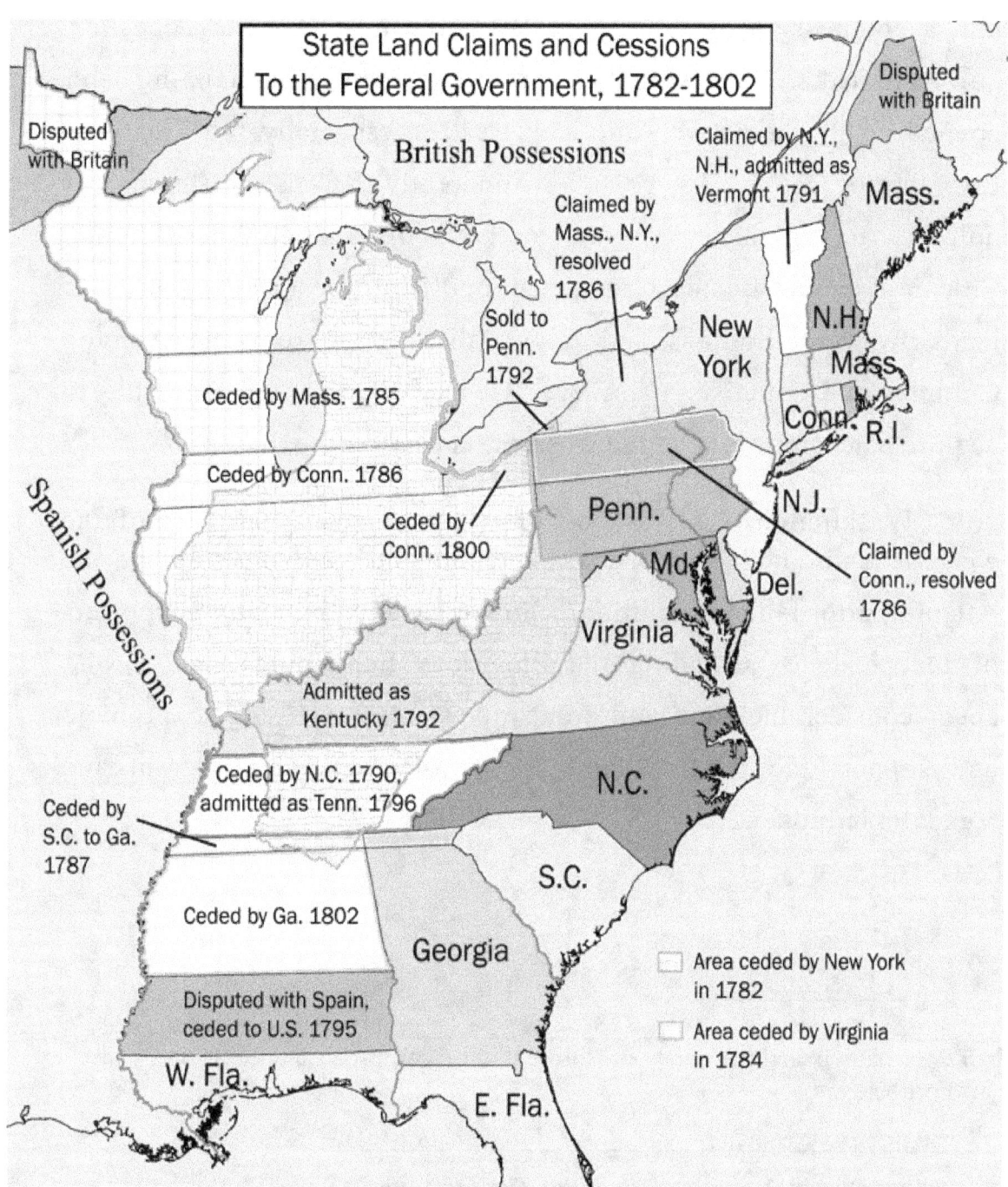

Map Showing Colonial Western Claims in 1763 Cut off by George III
.http://upload.wikimedia.org/wikipedia/commons/3/34/United_States_land_claims_and_cession
s_1782-1802.png

him a commission in the regular British army. One may question how satisfied he was with the new arrangements for claiming land opened up by the native American treaties, especially the Treaty of Lochaber of October 18, 1770.[236] Apparently there is a difference of opinion among historians as to how dissatisfied the Atlantic Colonials were with the Crown monopolizing the right to purchase lands from the Indians and taking that away from the Atlantic Colonies and colonists. However George Washington was able to acquire patents for land in the western lands after the treaties.[237]

Washington was just one of many illustrious seekers of the western lands, both supporters and opponents on both sides of the Atlantic, prior to the revolution, who were joined by many supporters of independence including the illustrious Benjamin Franklin who spent considerable time and some investment in trying to promote and support the western land claims of the Walpole grant and Vandalia in Indiana.[238]

---

[236] http://en.wikipedia.org/wiki/Treaty_of_Lochaber Other treaties were Treaty of Fort Stanwix and the Treaty of Hard Labour (both 1768) and the 1764 Treaty of Fort Niagara

[237] http://en.wikipedia.org/wiki/Royal_Proclamation_of_1763

[238] James Donald Anderson: *Vandalia: The First West Virginia?* West Virginia History Vol. 40, No. 4 (Summer 1979), pp. 375-92 http://en.wikipedia.org/wiki/Vandalia_(colony); http://founders.archives.gov/documents/Franklin/01-23-02-0094

The British crown had made a very clever land grab in 1763. George III declared on October 7, 1763[239] that as to all the western land acquired from the French:

"We have also thought fit, with the advice of our Privy Council as aforesaid, to give unto the Governors and Councils of our said Three new Colonies (Quebec, East Florida and West Florida), upon the Continent full Power and Authority to settle and agree with the Inhabitants of our said new Colonies or with any other Persons who shall resort thereto, for such Lands. Tenements and Hereditaments, as are now or hereafter shall be in our Power to dispose of; and them to grant to any such Person or Persons upon such Terms, and under such moderate Quit-Rents, Services and Acknowledgments, as have been appointed and settled in our other Colonies, and under such other Conditions as shall appear to us to be necessary and expedient for the Advantage of the Grantees, and the Improvement and settlement of our said Colonies."

There is no recognition of the claims of the original thirteen colonies to this land in this declaration. The proclamation went further and granted a reserve to the native Americans:

"And We do further declare it to be Our Royal Will and Pleasure, for the present as aforesaid, to reserve under our Sovereignty, Protection, and Dominion, for the use of the said

---

[239] http://avalon.law.yale.edu/18th_century/proc1763.asp

130

Indians, all the Lands and Territories not included within the Limits of Our said Three new Governments, or within the Limits of the Territory granted to the Hudson's Bay Company, as also all the Lands and Territories lying to the Westward of the Sources of the Rivers which fall into the Sea from the West and North West as aforesaid.

"And. We do further strictly enjoin and require all Persons whatever who have either wilfully or inadvertently seated themselves upon any Lands within the Countries above described. or upon any other Lands which, not having been ceded to or purchased by Us, are still reserved to the said Indians as aforesaid, forthwith to remove themselves from such Settlements."

So basically, the proclamation shut down all western claims of the Atlantic colonists at the headwaters of the Eastern rivers in the mountains, or at the crests of such chains as the Alleghenies. The entire Mississippi and Ohio River areas were gone from the wealth and potential tax base of the Thirteen Atlantic colonies and their land speculators..

The French Canadians were very upset with the proclamation of 1763 in the abolition of French civil law and barring the French Catholics from taking part in government. It contained elements that conflicted with the *Articles of Capitulation of Montreal*, granting Canadians the privilege of maintaining their civil laws and practice their religion. The application of British laws such as the penal Laws involved numerous administrative problems and legal irregularities. The requirements of the British Test Act of 1673,[240] mandating an oath that Catholics could not take, effectively excluded Catholics from administrative positions in the British Empire.[241]

The case for the Atlantic colonies was exacerbated by the Parliamentary act of 1774 which sought to resolve the French Canadian complains by revving French civil law in Quebec. This put the now very much expanded Quebec under the jurisdiction of a feudal civil law and authority..The King did promise warrants for lands to military veterans, but there may have been some problems with the exercise these warrants in the west.[242]

---

[240] 25 Car. II, ii

[241] http://en.wikipedia.org/wiki/Constitutional_history_of_Canada

[242] Maxwell, William B. "Washington's Western Lands." e-WV: The West Virginia Encyclopedia. 13 November 2013. Web. 01 February 2014. http://www.wvencyclopedia.org/articles/2344

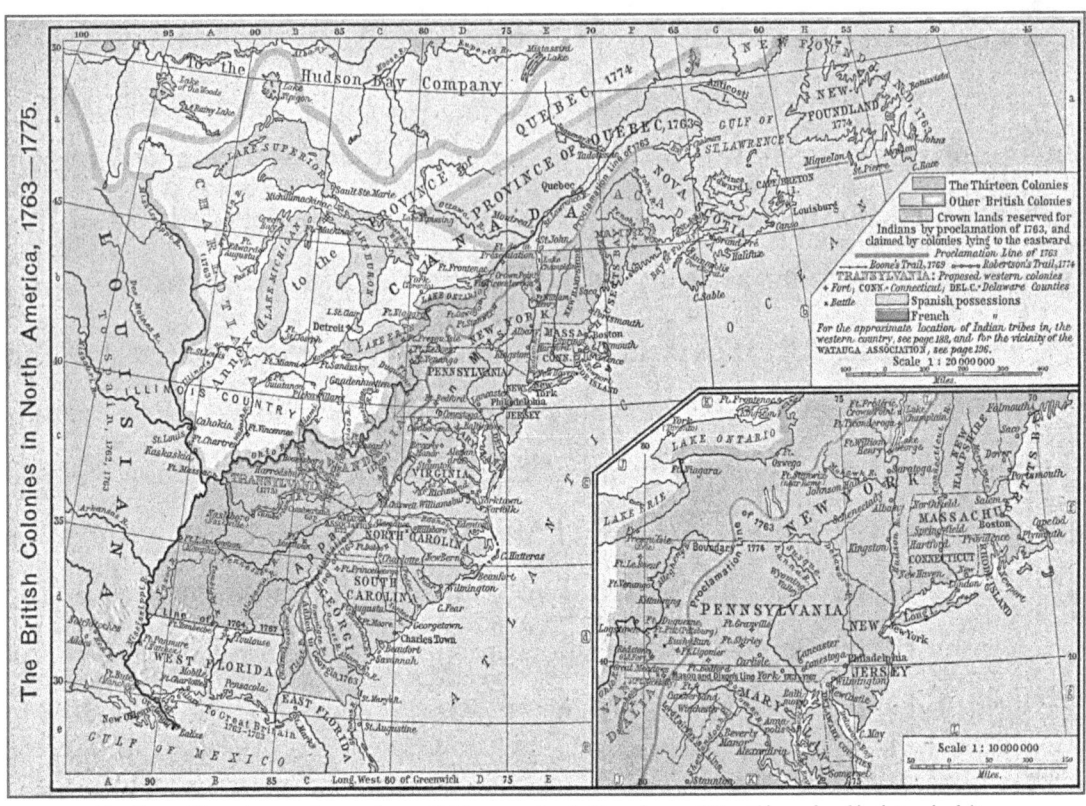

Indian Territory (grey) and Expanded Quebec (Outline in light pink)
http://en.wikipedia.org/wiki/File:British_ colonies_1763-76_shepherd1923.PNG
first published in: Shepherd, William Robert (1911) "The British Colonies
in North America, 1763–1765" in Historical Atlas, New York, United States:
Henry Holt and Company, pp. p. 194

George Washington, for example, was entitled to 5,000 acres of land under the proclamation, but never receive it until 1784 after the revolution. Probably most of the land that George Washington owned at his death, about 60,000 acres,[243] along with much of the land of his mentor Lord Fairfax, that was in West Virginia and was cut off by George III's 1763 proclamation. This would include their interests in the half million acres sought by the Ohio Company from before the French and Indian War. That financial loss, without even considering any slight he may have felt by never being given a regular commission in the British army, was more than enough to dispose George Washington to displeasure with George III and encourage him to assume command of the United Colonies' army outside of Boston in the American Colonial Revolution well before the Declaration of Independence. One could say that George Washington had a financial stake in joining the revolution, or in slang phraseology applicable to gamblers and speculators, skin in the game.

Western pressure of the expanding colonists caused the British government to seek to establish new boundaries with the native Americans that helped restore some of the land taken from the colonists that had been reserved to the various tribes. The 1768 treaty with the six Iroquois nations at Fort Stanwix, ceded the Kentucky portion, claimed by the Colony of Virginia, to the British,

---

[243] Ibid.

134

together with what is now West Virginia; was followed up by treaties of Hard Labour of 1770 with the Cherokee; The 1770 Treaty of Lochaber with the Cherokee; and the 1774 Treaty of Camp Charlotte with the Shawnee.[244] These did free up some western lands up to the new boundaries of the provinces of Quebec, East and West Florida and remaining Native American reserves, that might have been adjusted to recognize some of the Atlantic colonial claims, but perhaps too late. As the Declaration of Independence stated in reasons for independence:

> He has combined with others to subject us to a jurisdiction foreign to our constitution, and unacknowledged by our laws; giving his Assent to their Acts of pretended Legislation:...

> For abolishing the free System of English Laws in a neighbouring Province, establishing therein an Arbitrary government, and enlarging its Boundaries so as to render it at once an example and fit instrument for introducing the same absolute rule into these Colonies..

. In 1774 Parliament passed the Quebec Act[245] that reestablished French Civil law, with its seigneural system, in Quebec which now extended province's territory over part of the Indian Reserve, including much of what is now southern Ontario, Illinois, Indiana, Michigan, Ohio, Wisconsin, and parts of Minnesota. This effectively

---

[244] http://en.wikipedia.org/wiki/Treaty_of_Fort_Stanwix

[245] Quebec Act, 14 Geo. III c. 83

invalidated the Atlantic colonial land claims in the area[246] This could only exacerbate the wounds of the 1763 land grab by George III. The act in effect extended the French nobility - manorial system throughout the area.

Both British and Scots bought seigneurys in Quebec after the French ceded Canada to the British. For example, a British Army General from Scotland, Gabriel Christie (16 September 1722 – 26 January 1799) who settled in Montreal after the Paris peace treaty (1763), bought five seigneuries and invested in land to become one of the largest landowners in the British Province of Quebec (1763-1791).[247] His family continued to hold these properties until well after the end of the Seignuerial system. The seigneural manorial rights were used to control access to land, timber, mill sites, and other resources. Because of the increasing importance of these resources in the colonial economy, the seigneury itself continued to play a major economic roll in the Canadian colony.[248] Seigneural rights blended in promoting the newer capitalistic economies, proving there was not great distinctions between feudal power and later capitalistic power. Power is power and has obviously been up

---

[246] http://en.wikipedia.org/wiki/Quebec_Act

[247] http://search.findwide.com/serp?guid={D3B40CB8-7BA8-4CA5-A59B-3BB1 07B6DA2C}&action=default_search&serpv=22&k=Lieutenant-Colonel+Gabrie l+Christie

[248] Francoise No 1: Christie Seigneuries: Estate Management and Settlement in the Upper Richelieu Valley, 1760-1854, McGill-Queen's Press - MQUP, Apr 1, 1992

for sale since ancient times.   Money, wealth talks, to paraphrase recent Supreme Court case law.

Another example of British acquisition of seigneuries would be William Grant (June 15, 1744 – October 5, 1805).   He was a Scottish-born businessman, seigneur and political figure in Lower Canada. He acquired property in Quebec,[249] that included real estate at Saint-Roch.   He was able to have that designated a fief.   He also purchased a sub-fief known as La Mistanguienne (or Montplaisir) and the existing seigneury of Aubert-Gallion. Later, he purchased in 1779 the seigneury of Beaulac and part of Chambly; and after that acquired part of Île-d'Anticosti.

Even when the British began to create townships in Quebec after 1763, they continued to be referred to in official documents as in the western or "upper" part of Quebec as seigneuries until Upper Canada and Lower Canada were created from Quebec in 1791.[250]

---

[249] http://en.cyclopaedia.net/wiki/William-Grant-(seigneur); http://en.wikipedia.org/wiki/William_Grant_(seigneur).

[250] http://globalgenealogy.com/globalgazette/gazbm/gazbm057.htm

CHAPTER V

NOBILITY ABSOLUTELY BANNED

By revolutionary times there was a general fear in the Atlantic colonies of an established aristocracy, large disparities in social and economic distinctions and private governmental controls, an oligarchy. This may be observe from the state constitutions adopted at the time. **Pennsylvania in 1776** adopted its revolutionary state constitution clearly stating these principles. Article V of the Declaration of Rights provided:

> "That government is, or ought to be, instituted for the common benefit, protection and security of the people, nation or community; and not for the particular emolument or advantage of any single man, family, or set of men, who are a part only of that community; And that community hath an indubitable, unalienable and undefeasable right to reform, alter, or abolish government in such manner as shall be by that community judged most conducive to the public weal." [251]

The Pennsylvanians actually acted from such fears and confiscated the unimproved lands of the Proprietors, the Penn family. This was explained in a letter of James Tilghman to Lady Juliana Penn of August 14, 1782:

---

[251] http://avalon.law.yale.edu/18th_century/pa08.asp, Thorp, p 3082

"It was taken from the Proprietaries, not in a way of confiscation but upon principal of policy and expedience -- They thought the estate two [sic] large for a subject to posses, supposing it dangerous to the public that so much property should rest in the hands of one family."[252]

The Pennsylvanians also provided in their Constitution of 1790:

Article IX - That the general, great and essential principles of Liberty and free government may be recognized and unalterably established, we declare:

"1. That all men are born equally free and independent.... "

"2. That the legislature shall not grant any title of nobility or hereditary distinction, nor create any office the appointment of which shall be for a longer term than during good behavior."[253]

Pennsylvanians were not alone in fearing aristocracies and concentrations of power. In 1776 **North Carolina** adopted these provisions in her constitution:

"Article III: "That no man or set of men are entitled to exclusive or separate emoluments or privileges from the community, but in consideration of public services. "( )

Article XXII. That no hereditary emoluments, privileges or honors ought to be granted or conferred in this State.

[252] Shelburn Papers, 72:311; William L. Clements Library.

[253] Thorp: pp. 3093, 3099, 3101.

Article XXIII: "That perpetuities and monopolies are contrary to the genius of a free State, and ought not to be allowed." [254]

Maryland had similar fears and in the Declaration of Rights in her Constitution of 1776, she provided:

"Article XXXIX: "That monopolies are odious, contrary to the spirit of a free government, and the principles of commerce,

Article XL: "That no title of nobility, or hereditary honours, ought to be granted by this State."[255]

Massachusetts adopted her revolutionary constitution in 1780 and provided in Article VI in the Declaration of Rights:

"No man, nor corporation, or association of men, have any other title to obtain advantages, or particular and exclusive privileges, distinct from those of the community, than what arises from the consideration of services rendered to the public; and this title being in nature neither hereditary, nor transmissible to children, or descendants, or relations by blood, the idea of a man born a magistrate, lawgiver, or judge, is absurd and unnatural."[256]

---

[254] http://avalon.law.yale.edu/18th_century/nc07.asp, Thorp 2787, 2788.

[255] http://www.nhinet.org/ccs/docs/md-1776.htm Thorp....p. 1690

[256] http://en.wikisource.org/wiki/Constitution_of_the_Commonwealth_of_Massachusetts_ (1780)

This constitutional provision is credited with the remarkable jury instruction given by Chief Justice William Cushing in 1781 to the jury in the Worcester County Court of Common Pleas case which is a bundle of cases that have become collectively known as "the Quock Walker case," that spelled the death knell of slavery in Massachusetts confirmed in 1783. [257]

William Cushing (1732-1810) had been a member of the Massachusetts bar since 1755. He came from a line of judges in the colony and his father was an associate justice of the colonial Supreme Judicial Court from 1747-1771, when he resigned. On his resignation William Cushing was appointed in his place by the crown. Unlike the other crown appointed judges, William chose to go with the revolutionaries and became Chief Justice of the Supreme Judicial Court in 1777. He held this position until 1789 when he was the first associate justice nominated to the Supreme Court by George Washington. He served there for 21 years. Justice Cushing was considered for the Chief Justice which he declined for health reasons. He also served Vice-President of the Constitutional Convention of Massachusetts, in 1788, that ratified the United States Constitution.[258]

In 1781, still well within the spirit of the Revolution, William Cushing gave the following instruction on the new law since the

---

[257] The case was never set forth in the law reports, but was well covered in the press at the time. Douglass Harper. **Emancipation in Massachusetts**. http://slavenorth.com/massemancip.htm

[258] http://www.michaelariens.com/ConLaw/justices/cushing.htm

141

revolution to the jury in the case of <u>Commonwealth v. Jenneson</u> on the question of whether Quock Walker could be considered a slave in Massachusetts:

"As to the doctrine of slavery and the right of Christians to hold Africans in perpetual servitude, and sell and treat them as we do our horses and cattle, that (it is true) has been heretofore countenanced by the Province Laws formerly, but nowhere is it expressly enacted or established. It has been a usage -- a usage which took its origin from the practice of some of the European nations, and the regulations of British government respecting the then Colonies, for the benefit of trade and wealth. But whatever sentiments have formerly prevailed in this particular or slid in upon us by the example of others, a different idea has taken place with the people of America, more favorable to the natural rights of mankind, and to that natural, innate desire of Liberty, with which Heaven (without regard to color, complexion, or shape of noses-features) has inspired all the human race. And upon this ground our Constitution of Government, by which the people of this Commonwealth have solemnly bound themselves, sets out with declaring that all men are born free and equal -- and that every subject is entitled to liberty, and to have it guarded by the laws, as well as life and property -- and in short is totally repugnant to the idea of being born slaves. This being the case, I think the idea of slavery is inconsistent with our own conduct and Constitution; and there can be no such thing as perpetual servitude of a rational creature, unless his liberty is forfeited by some criminal conduct or given up by personal consent or contract ....,"[259]

The last case regarding slavery arose in September 1781, as part of the defense of Jenneson to an assault and battery charge brought against him for assaulting Walker. This case was filed by the Attorney General against Jennison, Commonwealth v. Jennison, for criminal assault and battery of Walker. In charging the jury, Chief Justice William Cushing stated:

"Without resorting to implication in constructing the constitution, slavery is...as effectively abolished as it can be by the granting of rights and privileges wholly incompatible and repugnant to its existence."[260]

This together with the contemporary case of Brom & Bett v. John Ashley, Esq. has been taken as setting the groundwork for the end of slavery in the state. On April 20, 1783, Jennison was found guilty and fined 40 shillings. The case is considered establishing the

---

[259] Proc. of Mass. Hist. Soc., Volume 1873-1875 Pages: p. 292-295.

[260] http://www.anti-slaverysociety.addr.com/hus-mass.htm

groundwork for the abolition of slavery in the State. The 1790 Federal Census recorded no slaves in Massachusetts.[261]

Vermont also joined the chorus of restricting special privileges in 1777:

Article VI: "That government is, or ought to be, instituted for the common benefit, protection, and security of the people, nations or community; and not for the particular emolument or advantage of any single man, family or set of men.... "

Article XXXIII: "As every freeman, to preserve his independence (if without sufficient estate) ought to have some profession, calling, trade or farm, whereby he may honestly subsist, there can be no necessity for, no use in establishing offices of profit, the usual effects of which are dependence and servility, unbecoming freemen, in the possessors or expectants; faction, contention, corruption and disorder among the people. But if any man is called into public service, to the prejudice of his private affairs, he has a right to a reasonable compensation; and whenever an office, through increase of fees; or otherwise, becomes so profitable as to occasion many to apply for it, the profits ought to be lessened by the legislature. "

---

[261] http://en.wikipedia.org/wiki/History_of_slavery_in_Massachusetts, http://www.masshist.org/endofslavery/index.php?id=54

Article XXXIV: "The future legislature of the State, shall regulate entails, in such manner as to prevent perpetuities."[262]

In February 5, 1777 **Georgia** agreed to an interesting twist to the legal literature for those who are interested in researching the equivalence of voting and citizenship rights.

"Nor shall any person who holds any title of nobility be entitled to vote, or be capable of serving as a representative, or hold any post of honor, profit, or trust in this State, whilst such person claims his title of nobility . . ."[263]

New York, in its constitution of April 20 1777, set forth the Declaration of Independence, and further made it clear:

"That all such parts of the said common law, and all such of the said statutes and acts aforesaid, or parts thereof, as may be construed to establish or maintain any particular denomination of Christians or their ministers, or concern the allegiance heretofore yielded to, and the supremacy, sovereignty, government, or prerogatives claimed or exercised by, the King of Great Britain and his predecessors, over the colony of New York and its inhabitants, or are repugnant to this constitution, be, and they hereby are, abrogated and rejected."[264]

---

[262] http://avalon.law.yale.edu/18th_century/vt01.asp Thorp p. 3740 et seq.

[263] Thorp...p.780

[264] (1777) http://www.nhinet.org/ccs/docs/ny-1777.htm, Thorp....p. 3813

This obviously covered sovereign grants of Titles of Nobility.

The people of **New Hampshire** were very strong in their Bill of Rights as written in 1784:

"IX. No office or place whatsoever in government, shall be hereditary -- the abilities and integrity requisite in all, not being transmissible to posterity or relations.

X. Government being instituted for the Common benefit, protection and security of the whole community, and not for the private interest or emolument of any one man, family or class of men. Therefore, whenever the ends of government are perverted, and public liberty manifestly endangered, and all other means of redress are ineffectual, the people may, and of right ought, to reform the old, or establish a new government. The doctrine of non-resistance against arbitrary power, and oppression, is absurd, slavish and destructive of the good and happiness of mankind."[265]

Virginia Bill of Rights, June 12, 1776:[266]

SECTION 1. "That all men are by nature equally free and independent, and have certain inherent rights, of which, when they enter into a state of society, they cannot, by any compact, deprive or divest their posterity, namely, the enjoyment of life

---

[265] Thorp.....p. 2455

[266] Thorp ,,,,p. 3818, http://www.nhinet.org/ccs/docs/va-1776.htm

and liberty, with the means of acquiring and possessing property, and pursuing and obtaining happiness and safety.

SEC. 4. That no man, or set of men, are entitled to exclusive or separate emoluments or privileges from the community, but in consideration of public services; which, not being descendible, neither ought the offices of magistrate, legislator, or judge to be hereditary.

In the Virginia Constitution:

A Governor, or chief magistrate....shall not, under any presence, exercise any power or prerogative, by virtue of any law, statute or custom of England.

So he cannot grant any feudal rights or title os nobility

All escheats, penalties, and forfeitures, heretofore going to the King, shall go to the Commonwealth, save only such as the Legislature may abolish, or otherwise provide for. Land continues to be held in the Fee, feudal style and no titles recognized in any allodial form, independent of any superior landlord. However they now said that the land reverts to the people of Virginia and not to some prior lord or king..

In **South Carolina's** third Constitution of 1790, she observed the trend:

"Article IX. Sec. 5. The legislature shall not grant any title of nobility, or hereditary distinction, nor create any office the appointment to which shall be for any longer time than during good behavior."[267]

By 1792 **Delaware** had Joined the chorus:

*Sec. 19: No hereditary distinction shall be granted, nor any office created or exercised, the appointment to which shall be for a longer term than during good behavior; and no person holding any office under this State shall accept of any office or title of any kind whatever, from any king, prince, or foreign state."

Delaware continues:

"We declare that everything in this article is reserve out of the general powers of government hereinafter mentioned."[268]

Maine was admitted in 1820 and its constitution, Article section 23 provided:

"No title of Nobility or hereditary distinction, privilege, honor or emolument, shall ever be granted or confirmed, nor shall any office be created, the appointment to which shall be longer time than during good behavior."[269]

How much this reminds us of the expression of reservations of certain powers as set forth over a century before in **The Agreement**

---

[267] Thorp.... p. 3264

[268] Thorp.....p. 570

[269] Thorp.... p. 1648

of the Free People of England proposed in 1648 as the revolution overthrew Charles I, by granting general powers to Parliament subject to enumerated reservations:

> "VII. That the power of the People's Representatives extend (without the consent or concurrence of any other person or persons) to the enacting, altering, repealing, and declaring of laws; to the erecting and abolishing officers of courts of justice, and to whatsoever is not in this Agreement excepted or reserved from them."

As particularly:

> "1. We do not empower our Representatives to continue in force, or make, any laws, oaths, covenants, whereby to compel by penalties or otherwise any person to anything in or about matters of faith, religion, or God's worship, or to restrain any person from the professing his faith, or exercise of religion according to his conscience in any house or place (except such as are, or shall be, set apart for public worship); nevertheless the instruction or directing of the nation in a public way for the matters of faith, worship, or discipline (so it be not compulsive or express popery) is referred to their discretion.
>
> 2. We do not empower them to impress or constrain any person to serve in war either by sea or land, every man's conscience being to be satisfied in the justness of that cause where he hazards his life.

3. That after the dissolution of this present Parliament, none of the people be at any time questioned for anything said or done in reference to the late wars or public differences, otherwise than in the execution or pursuance of the determination of the present House of Commons against such as have adhered to the King or his interest against the people; and saving that accomptants (sic) for public moneys received, shall remain accomptable for the same.

4 That in any laws hereafter to be made, no person by virtue of any tenure, grant, charter, patent, degree or birth, shall be privileged from subjection thereto, or (from) being bound thereby as well as others.

5. That all privileges or exemptions of any persons from the laws, or from the ordinary course of legal proceedings, by virtue of any tenure, grant, charter, patent, degree or birth, or of any place of residence or refuge, shall be henceforth void and null, and the like not be made nor revived again.

6 . That the Representatives intermeddle not with the execution of laws, or give judgement upon any man's person or estate, where no law bath been before provided, save only in calling to an accompt, and punishing public officers for abusing or failing their trust.

7   That no member of any future Representative be made either receiver, treasurer or other officer during that employment, saving to be a member of the Council of State.

8 .   That no Representative shall in any wise render up, or give, or take away any the foundations of common right, liberty or safety contained in this Agreement, nor shall level Ten's estates, destroy propriety (sic), or make all things common."[270]

Are we not finding a continual reaffirmation of those basic rights and social formation of government as set forth for the world on June 12, 1776 in the Bill of Rights of the Constitution of Virginia:

"Section 1. That all men are by nature equally free and independent, and have certain inherent rights, of which, when they enter into a state of society, they cannot, by any compact, deprive or divest their posterity; namely, the enjoyment of life and liberty, with the means of acquiring and possessing property, and pursuing and obtaining happiness and safety.

Section 2. That all power is vested in, and consequently derived from, the people; that magistrates are their trustees and servants, and at all times amenable to them.

---

[270] Woodhouse **Puritanism and Liberty** supra p. 360, being a part of the Second Agreement of the People (1648) from John Lilburn **Foundations of Freedom**

Section 3. That government is, or ought to be, instituted for the common benefit, protection, and security of the people, nation, or community; of all the various modes and forms of government, that is best which is capable of producing the greatest degree of happiness and safety, and is most effectually secured against the danger of maladministration; and that, when any government shall be found inadequate or contrary to these purposes, a majority of the community hath an indubitable, inalienable, and indefeasible right to reform, alter, or abolish it, in such manner as shall be judged most conducive to the public weal.

Section 4. That no man, or set of men, are entitled to exclusive or separate emoluments or privileges from the community, but in consideration of public services; which, not being descendible, neither ought the offices of magistrate, legislator, or judge to be hereditary." [271]

It should hardly surprise us, therefore, that when the **Articles of Confederation**, our first national Constitution, was proposed in 1777 and adopted in 1781, it contained this language:

"Article VI: . . nor shall any person holding any office of profit or trust under the United States, or any of them, accept any present, emolument, office, or title of any kind whatever from any king, prince or foreign state; nor shall the United

---

[271] Thorp 3813

152

States in Congress assembled, or any of them, grant any title of nobility."[272]

Considering that neither **Rhode Island** nor **Connecticut** needed new revolutionary Constitutions, these show sentiments against Nobility and its class distinctions were widely, nearly universally accepted by the revolutionaries as fundamental at the time.

William Rawle, Philadelphia lawyer, U.S. Attorney, and first person to write a treaties on the constitution, offers us no particular understanding of the clauses in his cryptic comment in 1725:

"No title of nobility shall be granted by the United States, or by any individual states. Of this there could have been but little danger. The independent spirit of republicans lead them to contemn the variety of hereditary distinctions,...."[273]

Is it any wonder that Justice Story identified these nobility restrictions with the existence of a perfect equality as the basis for all our institutions and that this prohibited distinctions between citizens in regard to rank in order to avoid laying foundations of

---

[272] **Documents Illustrative of The Foundation of the Union of American States** (69th Congress, 1st Session House Document No. 378) p. 29

[273] William Rawle, LL.B., **A View of the Constitution of the United States** 2nd Ed. 1829, p. 119.

odious claims and privilege that could silently subvert the spirit of independence and personal dignity of the people.[274]

Was not constitutional scholar Joel Tiffany making a reasonably logical conclusion that this took from the government the right to create classes or class distinctions among the people and that all laws are enacted in the hypothesis that all men are created equal and equally entitled at the hands of their government.[275]

Thus is it any surprise that the Supreme Court of Errors in Connecticut would say, in considering a similar clause in Connecticut's first State Constitution of 1818:

"The 'legislative power of this state' is, in the broadest terms, vested in the 'general assembly'. This power is, in a certain way, defined and limited by the provisions dividing the powers of government into distinct departments, and by those relating to the operation of the state government and duties of particular officers. But, unlike the Constitution of many states, it contains no specific limitations on the exercise of legislative power, except some slight restrictions in one or two recent amendments. The limitations, however, are no less real and perhaps more effective, than if phrased in specific terms. Our Bill of Rights constitutes the fundamental condition on

---

[274] Joseph Story **Commentaries on the Constitution of The United States** Sections 1350, 1351 (Fifth edition 1891, Vol. II, Ch. XXXII, p. 223)

[275] Joel Tiffany **A Treatise on Government and Constitutional Law** (1867) Section 476, p. 297

154

which all powers of government can be exercised. Its more definite declarations are chiefly concerned with the administration of justice, especially of the criminal law, the preservation of the trial by jury, the protection of private property from confiscation for public use, the right of the citizen to bear arms, and the subordination of the military to the civil power; but the protection of the citizen in the equal enjoyment of those essential rights belonging to citizens of a free government is guaranteed, not in narrow phrases of detailed statement, but in terms as broad as those which vest the legislative power in the general assembly or the judicial power in the courts. The Bill of Rights begins as follows: 'That the great and essential principles of liberty and free government may be recognized and established, we declare that all men when they form a social compact are equal in rights; and that no man or set of men are entitled to exclusive public emoluments or_ privileges from the community.' No legislative act is law that clearly and certainly is obnoxious to the principle of equality in rights thus solemnly made the condition of all exercise of legislative power."[276]

In July, 1776 we were over one year into an open Continental-Atlantic armed revolution that had just formally turned into a war of independence. We were actively denying to ourselves, in setting up

---

[276] State v. Colon 65 Conn. 478, 33A. 519, 31 L.R.A. 55, 48 Am. St. Rep. 227 (1895)

our basic laws, any oligarchical aristocracy in favor of a higher equality above which none would be allowed to rise through the pubic trust or confirmation. One obvious aristocracy was the British eighteenth century aristocracy that could act as the leader and protector of the country. We would not allow the existence of those whom Burke would call "the great oakes that shade a country ..."

"You people, of great families and hereditary trusts and fortunes are not like such as I am, who, whatever we may be by the rapidity of our growth, and even by the fruit we bear, and flatter ourselves that, while we creep on the ground, we belly into melons that are exquisite for size and flavour, yet still we are but annual plants that perish with our season, and leave no sort of traces behind us. You, if you are what you ought to be, are in my eye the great oaks that shade a country, and perpetuate your benefits from generation to generation. The immediate power of a Duke of Richmond, or a Marquis of Rockingham, is not so much of moment; but if their conduct and example hand down their principles to their successors, then their houses become the public repositories and office of record for the constitution.... I do not look upon your time or lives as lost, if in this sliding away from the genuine spirit of the country, certain parties, if possible--if not, the heads of certain families--should make it their business by the whole course of their lives, principally by their example, to mould into the very vital stamina of their descendants those principles which ought to be transmitted pure and unmixed to posterity."[277]

Now new ideas and new options were loose in the world. Thomas Paine felt able to propose a 10% death duty to compensate the landless population for the loss.[278] It is still a reasonable proposal because it is through the application of law recognizing statutory dissent an distributions, wills and trusts and placing land in the ownership of corporations that may have no death that the states provide for the concentration through inheritances of power and wealth from generation to generation. Inheritance requires the positive activity of the state whether by descent and distribution statutes in cases of intestacy, or by wills, or trusts that must be recognized by the state. This was confirmed by Mr. Justice Jackson in Irving Trust Co. v. Day (1942):[279]

> " Rights succession to property of a deceased, whether by will or intestacy, are of statutory creation, and the dead hand rules succession only by sufferance' Nothing in the Federal Constitution forbids the legislature of a state to limit,

---

[277] *Letter to Duke of Richmond* (November 17, 1772) http://www.fullbooks.com/Burke1.html **Letters of Edmund Burke a selection**, No. 155. Henry Library /World Classics, CCXXVII Edited, with introduction by Harold J. Laski. See also **The Political Economy of Edmund Burke, The Role of Property in His Thought** by Francis Canavan (195) p 82-83

[278] Thomas Paine pamphlet **Agrarian Justice**, 1797 English translation. http://www.ssa.gov/history/tpaine3.html

[279] Irving Trust Co. v. Day (1942) 314 U,S, 586, 86 L.Ed. 1734, 62 S.Ct. 398, 137 ALR 1093:

condition or even abolish the power of testamentary disposition over property within its jurisdiction. <u>Mages v. Grima</u>. 8 How (U.S.) 490. 12 L.Ed. 1168; <u>United States v. Fox</u>, 94 U.S. 315, 24 L.Ed. 192; <u>United States v. Perkins</u>, 163 U.S. 625, 41 L.Ed. 287, 16 S.Ct. 1073; cf. <u>Randall v. Kreiger</u>, 23 Wall (U.S.) 137, 148, 23 L.Ed. 124, 126..

At the point of death, the deceased's property can only be transferred by will, intestate decent or trust and all require the positive acknowledgment and protection of the state to take place. Otherwise the deceased's property no longer belongs to anyone. Prior to 1066 cE with William the Conquer's introduction of his Feudalism to England, in many parts of England the land and property reverted to the community upon death. So that is not a new idea in our cultural history. In its natural state, at death the possessions are up for grabs to the strongest or most assertive. To the victor belongs the spoils. Can the general population be victorious, or are we to assume that the oligarchy triumphed?

If nobility is defined as inheriting certain level of economic power, then this could well be labeled a grant of a title of nobility because the state's action of approval of that unequal, superior power personal inheritance, is the granting the title and all associated rights an property. Presumably both the State and Federal government's could establish parameters to such dispositions, as the restrictions apply equally to both. These ideas were not foreign to people at the time of the revolution. A Scottish professor, William

Ogilvie, would in 1781 attack the landowners' "pernicious monopoly" of the soil and proposed an agricultural law of government purchase and wide redistribution of the land..[280]

The Pennsylvanians could confiscate the unsettled land of William Penn, not in the name of independence but in the fear of an aristocracy. Thomas Smith, a conservative with the view of a minority member of the Pennsylvania Constitutional Convention could observe of the moving impulses of the times in a letter of August 3, 1776:

> "It is not only that their notions are original, but they would go to the devil for popularity, and in order to acquire it, they have embraced levelling principles, which you know is a fine method of succeeding. Don't therefore, be surprised if in the next letter I write you, I should inform you that we had passed an Agrarian law."[281]

The "Agrarian Law" was a pejorative term of the day more attuned to our use of "socialism" and even "communism" today.

If some of our comments look like a rehash of Fourteenth Amendment equal protection of the laws position, it is well to reflect that even as this is written, the Federal courts have been reluctant to apply equal protection requirements to the action of the Federal

---

[280] G. F. Mingay **English Landed Society** p. 267

[281] *Thomas Smith to Maj. General Arthur St. Clair.* **St. Clair Papers,** William Henry Smith, editor (Robert Clark Co. 1882) Vol. I, p. 371

government. However, the courts and the lawyers have attempted to find reasoning, most circuitously through the Fifth Amendment, to apply equal protection to some Federal action in the absence of some ill-defined national policies to the contrary. [282]

The cynic might wonder if the observation in the second volume of the American Law Journal in 1809 set the tone for the silence of the bar and the courts concerning the significance of the nobility clauses. Lawyers make good income from will, trusts, corporation, probate and estate work. In the author's biographical sketch of the Right Honorable Lord Chancellor Eldon (Sir John Scott) he noted: "Nearly one—third of the whole nobility of England are either lawyers or descendants of lawyers."[283]

For whatever reason, despite the most detailed examination of almost every other letter, punctuation mark, and clause of the Constitution by generations of judges, legal scholars and historians, it may be fairly safely said today, after almost two hundred and forty years, most judges and lawyers in this country are unaware of the existence of the nobility restriction in the United States Constitution. Or if they knew the clauses exist, they have no idea of what they prohibit. Such is the present resting place of the cornerstone of our republican

---

[282] For analysis of this circuitous reasoning see Kenneth L. Karst *The Fifth Amendment Guarantee of Equal Protection*, N.C.L. Rev. 55:541 (April 1977) As we can see from these comments, circuitous reasoning allowing wide judicial discretion of whether apply equal protection of the *laws* is not necessary.

[283] American Law Journal 2:484 (1809)

government, lost and forgotten like that of the United States Capital. But there are a couple of more recent exceptions, Jol A. Silversmith and Richard Delgado.[284] Silversmith observed: in his article last updated in 2005:

> "We should remember that the nobility clauses were adopted because the founders were concerned not only about the bestowal of titles but also about an entire social system of superiority and inferiority, of habits of deference and condescension, of social rank, and political, cultural and economic privilege--a system of inequality that some commentators argue is reemerging."

In other words, these clauses appear to limit the inequality at the top, the disparities of wealth an power. Cynics may further suggest that this is the primary reason they have had little application, enforcement or serious legal or political discussion.

Another recent writer on the subject commented

"In determining then, whether the anti-nobility clauses might have an application in modern American society, we must consider whether arrangements presently exist, or are contemplated, which partake of one or more of these elements: 1) perpetual or hereditary transmission; 2) private ownership and

---

[284] Jol A. Silversmith, *Missing Thirteenth Amendment": Constitutional Nonsense and Titles of Nobility.* 8 **Southern California Interdisciplinary Law Journal** 577 (April 1999) and Richard Delgado, *Inequality "From the Top": Applying an Ancient Prohibition to an Emerging Problem of Distributive Justice*, 32 **UCLA L. Rev.** 100, 114 (1984).

control over common heritage resources (natural resources which were not humanly produced); 3) disproportionate influence in the political process; 4) favoritism in criminal or civil judicial processes; and 5) reduction in national allegiance on the part of the benefitted parties. [285]

Our historical desire to restrict oligarchy, aristocracy was old at the time the more historically remembered causes of the American revolution occurred. But we often forget that until we did revolt we were Englishmen, and our history was English history and that we had revolted again in 1775 as Englishmen before declaring Independence..

The aversion to any aristocracy could be found in the work of a member of Lincoln's Inn, Anthony Wood, barrister who was also secretary to the parliamentary army under the Earl of Essex. In 1650 this English republican wrote:

"It cannot be rationally or spiritually supposed, that any man should be born a magistrate or governor, especially not successively; when the best men and choice spirits, who have *had* the *highest* eminences of virtue and best improvements of education and natural genius, are hardly fit for so great a work."[286]

---

[285] **Intergenerational Justice in the United States Constitution, The Stewardship Doctrine: III. Constitutional Text**, B *Prohibitions of Nobility - modern American society.* Constitutional Law Foundation, 50 West 36th Street, Eugene, Oregon 97405 http://www.conlaw.org/Intergenerational-III-2-4.htm

[286] Somers Collection cif Tracts (2nd Ed. London 1818 Vol. VI) *The True Portraiture of Kings of England •..*, p. 82 (this selection did not appear in the

As Englishmen we had revolted for many of the same causes a century and a quarter before, but the revolt had been aborted by Cromwell and his backing in the New Model Army. Yet before the revolt was aborted, in 1647-1648, written constitutions for the people of England were proposed. One of these proposed constitution was entitled "An Agreement of the Free People of England" proposed, among its provisions:

> "That all privileges or exemptions of any persons from Lawes, or from the ordinary course of Legal proceedings, by virtue of any Tenure, Grant, Charter, Patent, Decree, or Birth, or any place of residence, or refuge, or privilege of Parliament, shall be henceforth void and nul, and the like not to be made or revived again."[287]

first edition available to the American revolutionary)

[287] William Haller and Godfrey Davis, ed. **The Leveller Tracts 1647-1653** (1944) p. 318 et. Seq. This remarkable document went through several editions during the time and can be found in various forms in a number of works available to study today. In addition to the foregoing one can find it in number 26 of the **Old South Leaflets**. Student editions including Leveller works can be found in Samuel Rawson Gardner's **The Constitutional Documents of the Puritan Revolution 1625-1660** (3rd revised ed. Oxford University press reprint 1968); J. P. .Kenyon **The Stuart Constitutional Documents and Commentary** (Cambridge University Press reprint 1973); A. L. Morton, ed. **Freedom in Arms** (Lawwrence & Wishart, ltd. London 1975; A.S.P. Woodhouse **Puritanism and Liberty** (2nd ed. J.M. Dent & Sons, Ltd. 1974 (also contains the Putney Debates); and Don M. Wolf, **The Leveler Manifestos of the Puritan Revolution** (T. Nelson and Sons, 1944)

Certainly some, at the time, felt close kinship to the English revolution. In an extract from a letter dated August 17, 1776, at Staten Island, the writer said:

"It is now the Puritan's high holiday season, and they enjoy it with rapture all over the continent. Their behavior exactly assimilates the manners of the king-killing tribe during the English grand rebellion."[288]

The ghost of the nobility restrictions survived long enough to be included in Article 1, section 7 (8) of the Provisional Constitution of the Confederate States of America [289] and again in Article 1, Section 9(54) {11} of the Constitution of the Confederate States of America..[290]

Spirit of the Law

There are indications from the Supreme Court that should imply that the nobility restrictions are part of our basic law. Observe this holding in the case from the United States Supreme Court in the court's opinion in the case of Carter v. Carter Coal Co. (1936):

"in the very nature of things, one person may not be entrusted with the power to regulate the business of another, and especially

---

[288] Frank V. Moore **Diary of The American Revolution** (New York 1865) Vol I p.291

[289]

http://www.csawardept.com/documents/Constitutions/CSA/Provisional/index.html

[290] Charles Robert Lee, Jr. **The Confederate Constitutions** (1963) p. 163et seq. And 183 et seq.

of a competitor. And a statute which attempts to confer such power undertakes an intolerable and unconstitutional interference with personal liberty and private property. "[291]

Was it considering the heritage of the Nobility clauses, as this action is far from slavery outlawed by the thirteenth amendment, and taking of property without just compensation under the fifth amendment. The Supreme Court has no authority to rule against a practice unlawful or unconstitutional merely because it may find it just intolerable.

---

[291] Carter v. Carter Coal Co., (1936) 298 U.S. 238, 311–12. 56 S.Ct. 855. 80 L.Ed. 1160

CHAPTER VI

ARGUMENTS ON CONSTITUTIONAL ADOPTION

Hereditary descent was not the only objectionable accouterment of nobility, nor even a necessary ingredient. Yet it played an important role as can be seen from these passages by Thomas Paine in Common Sense:

"First. - the remains of Monarchial tyranny in the person

of the King.

Second. - the remains of Aristocratical tyranny in the

person of the Peers

The two first by being hereditary are independent of the

People; wherefore in a constitutional sense they con

tribute nothing towards the freedom of the State. (8)

For all men being originally equals, no one by birth

could have a right to set up his own family in perpetual

preference to all others forever, and tho' himself might

deserve some honoure of his contemporaries, yet his

descendants might be far too untrustworthy to inherit

them.[292]

---

[292]

http://www.earlyamerica.com/earlyamerica/milestones/commonsense/text.html

Most wise men in their private sentiments have ever

treated hereditary right with contempt; yet it is one of

those evils, which once established is not easily removed:

many submit from fear, others from superstition, and

the more powerful part shares with the King the plunder

of the rest."[293]

The fear of establishment of an aristocracy continued throughout the period of the confederacy (1781-1789) preceding the Constitutional Convention (May 25 to September 17, 1787). This can be seen in a reply reply to the Massachusetts legislature on its instructions to introduce a resolution in the Continental Congress calling for a Constitutional Convention. The Massachusetts delegates warned:

"What the effect then may be of calling a Convention to revise the Confederation generally, we leave with your Excellency and the honorable Legislature to determine. We are apprehensive and it is our duty to declare it, that such a measure would produce thro-out the Union, an exertion of the friends of an aristocracy to send members who would promote a change of government, and we can form some judgment of the plan such members would report to Congress.... "

"More power in Congress has been the cry from all quarters, but especially of those whose views, not being confined

---

[293] Ibid

to a government that will promote the happiness of the people, are extended to one that will afford lucrative employments, civil and military. Such a government is an aristocracy, which would require a standing army and a numerous train of pensioners and placemen to prop and support its exalted administration. To recommend one's self to such an administration would be to secure an establishment for life and at the same time to provide for his posterity. These are pleasing prospects, which republican governments do not afford. "[294]

The ingredients for the establishment of an aristocracy did appear to exist at the time. Louis Guillaume Otto, French Consul to New York, commented in a letter of October, 1786 to Count Vergennes, the French Foreign Minister, concerning the Annapolis Convention:

"Although there are no nobles in America, there is a class of men denominated 'gentlemen' who, by reason of their wealth, their talents, their education, their families, of the offices they hold, aspire to preeminence which the people refuse to grant them; and, although many of these men have betrayed the interests of their order to gain popularity, there reigns among them a connection so much the more intimate as they almost all of them dread the efforts of the people to despoil them of their possessions, and,

---

[294] *Inquiry Into the Origin and Course of Political Parties in the United States* Author: Martin Van Buren Editor: Abraham Van Buren John Van Buren Release Date: April 22, 2011 [EBook #35932] pp. 42-43
http://www.gutenberg.org/files/35932/35932-h/35932-h.htm

moreover, they are creditors, and therefore, interested in strengthening the government, and watching over the execution of the laws."[295]

Indeed, Richard Henry Lee[296] described the existence of the American aristocracy in his writings opposing adoption of the new constitution. He was arguably the best known Antifederalist writer. His pamphlets were widely distributed and reprinted in newspapers. Here is an excerpt from his work:

> The Eastern states [New England] are very democratic, and composed chiefly of moderate freeholders; they have but few rich men and no slaves; the Southern states are composed chiefly of rich planters and slaves; they have but few moderate freeholders, and the prevailing influence in them is generally a dissipated aristocracy. The Middle states partake partly of the Eastern and partly of the Southern character. . . ."[297]

---

[295] John H. Ferguson and Dean L. Henry, **The American System of Government** (1953) p.25, George Bancroft, **History of the Formation of the Constitution**, vol. ii, Appendix, pp. 399-400. See also http://www.earlyamerica.com/ebooks/books/FathersOfConstitution/FathersOfConstitution.html

[296] Richard Henry Lee (January 20, 1732 – June 19, 1794) was an American statesman from Virginia best known for the motion in the Second Continental Congress calling for the colonies' independence from Great Britain. He descended from an ancient and distinguished family in Virginia.

[297] Antifederalist Papers, Gary Shade: No. 36 *Representation and Internal Taxation*. http://www.firearmsandliberty.com/AntiFederalist/TheAntiFederalistPapers.pdf

After the Constitution was proposed and during the period of its debate it was regularly challenged from fear that its adoption would lead to the establishment of an aristocracy. Many proponents and opponents used pseudonyms (such as a "Federal Farmer " used by Richard Henry Lee), thus it is not always possible to identify the real author of the articles.

There was great secrecy surrounded the drafting of the Constitution. Indeed, the notes on the convention were not to be published for many years. This in itself raised considerable suspicion as pointed out by "A Federalist" writing in the Boston Gazette and County Journal on November 26, 1787.

> "It will first be allowed that many undersigning citizens may wish its adoption from the best of motives, but these are modest and silent, when compared to the greater number, who endeavor to suppress all attempts for investigation. These violent partisans arc for having the people gulp down the gilded pill blindfolded, whole, and without any qualification whatever. These consist of the NOBLE order of C(incinnatu)s, holders of public securities, men of great wealth and expectations of public office, B(an)k(er)s and L(aw)y(er)s: these with their train of dependents form an Aristocratic combination. "[298]

---

[298] **AntiFederalist Paper No. 1** General Introduction: *A Dangerous Plan of Benefit Only to the Aristocratick Combination* From The Boston Gazette and Country Journal, November 26, 1787
http://www.rightsofthepeople.com/freedom_documents/anti_federalist_papers/anti_federalist_papers_01.php

Some of the published objections to the 'proposed new Constitution fearing the establishment of an order of Aristocracy' engaged in satire to convey their points. This may be witnesses from these comments of "Montezuma" appearing in the (Philadelphia) Independent Gazetteer of October 17, 1787:

> "We the Aristocratic party of the United States, lamenting the many inconveniences to which the late confederation subjected the well-born, the better kind of people, bringing them down to the level of the rabble-and holding in utter detestation that frontispiece to every bill of rights, "that all men are born equal" - beg leave (for the purpose of drawing a line between such as we think were ordained to govern, and such as were made to bear the weight of government without having any share in its administration) to submit to our Friends in the first class for their inspection, the following defense of our monarchical, aristocratical democracy...
>
> 1st, As a majority of all societies consist of men who (though totally incapable of thinking or acting in governmental matters) are more readily led than driven, we have thought meet to indulge them in something like a democracy in the new constitution, which part we have designated by the popular name of the House of Representatives. But to guard against every possible danger from this lower house, we have subjected every bill they bring

forward to the double negative of our upper house and president."[299]

We must remember that the Constitution did not assure direct election of Senators until ratification of the 17th Amendment adopted in 1913.

The proposed Constitution was often attacked, as in Pennsylvania, as setting up an aristocracy:

"In many of the states, particularly in this [Pennsylvania] and the northern states, there are aristocratic juntos of the well-horn few, who have been zealously endeavoring since the establishment of their constitutions, to humble that offensive upstart, equal liberty; but all their efforts were unavailing, the ill-bred churl obstinately kept his assumed station . . .

A comparison of the authority under which the convention acted, and their form of government, will show that they have despised their delegated power, and assumed sovereignty; that they have entirely annihilated the old confederation, and the particular governments of the several States, and instead thereof have established one general government that is to pervade the union; constituted on the most unequal principles, destitute of accountability to its constituents, and as despotic in its nature, as

[299] **Antifederalist Paper No. 9** — *A Consolidated Government Is a Tyranny*
http://www.thefederalistpapers.org/antifederalist-paper-9

the Venetian aristocracy; a government that will give full scope to the magnificent designs of the well-horn, a government where tyranny may glut its vengeance on the low-born, unchecked by an odious bill of rights. . . ; and yet as a blind upon the understandings of the people, they have continued the forms of the particular governments, and termed the whole a confederation of the United States, pursuant to the sentiments of that profound, but corrupt politician Machiavel, who advises any one who would change the constitution of a state to keep as much as possible to the old forms; for then the people seeing the same officers, the same formalities, courts of justice and other outward appearances, are insensible of the alteration, and believe themselves in possession of their old government. Thus Caesar, when he seized the Roman liberties, caused himself to be chosen dictator (which was an ancient office), continued the senate, the consuls, the tribunes, the censors, and all other offices and forms of the commonwealth; and yet changed Rome from the most free, to the most tyrannical government in the world . . ."[300]

This appeared in the Independent Gazettet of Philadelphia on October 5, 1787 and is attributed to Samuel Bryan, the son of George Bryan, one of the authors of the Pennsylvania Constitution.[301]

---

[300] **Antifederalist** No. 40 ***On the Motivations and Authority of the Founding Fathers***
http://www.rightsofthepeople.com/freedom_documents/anti_federalist_papers/anti_federalist_papers_40.php

[301] "Centinel" http://www.constitution.org/afp/centin00.htm

Nor was looking at aristocracy only to be found in examination of the monarchy or House of Lords:

"A democratic branch market with strong features of aristocracy, and an aristocratic branch with all the impurities and imperfections of the British House of Commons, arising from the inequality of representation and want of responsibility."

This was also observed by Mr. William Grayson (1740 – March 12, 1790) in his comments on the proposed constitution to the Virginia Convention.[302]

Richard Henry Lee, on October 10, 1787, perceived the tendency towards an aristocracy in the executive:

". . . but when we examine the powers of the president, and the forms of the executive, we shall perceive that the general government, in this part, will have a strong tendency to aristocracy, or the government of a few. "[303]

George Mason, a Virginia delegate to the Constitutional Convention in giving his reasons for not signing the proposed Constitution predicted dire consequences under the new government:

---

[302] **The Debates in the Several State Conventions on the Adoption of the Federal Constitution** 2d Ed Vol III, Jonathan Elliot *The Debates in the Convention of the Commonwealth of Virginia, On the Adoption of the Federal Constitution. June 11, 1788,*, P. 280
http://www.constitution.org/rc/rat_va_09.htm

[303] Letters from the Federal Farmer to the Republican III October 10th, 1787.
http://www.constitution.org/afp/fedfar03.txt

"This government will commence in a moderate aristocracy; it is at present impossible to foresee whether it will, in its operation, produce a monarchy, or a corrupt, oppressive aristocracy; it will most probably vibrate some years between the two, and then terminate in one or the other."[304]

More of this wide fear is indicated by the words of Melancton Smith to the New York Convention:

"Besides, the influence of the great will generally enable them to succeed in elections--it will be difficult to combine a district of country containing 30 or 40,000 inhabitants, frame your election laws as you please, in any one character; unless it be in one of conspicuous, military, popular, civil or legal talents. The great easily form associations; the poor and middling class form them with difficulty. If the elections be by plurality, as probably will be the case in this state, it is almost certain, none but the great will be chosen--for they easily unite their interest--The common people will divide, and their divisions will be promoted by the others. There will be scarcely a chance of their uniting, in any other but some great man, unless in some popular demagogue, who will probably be destitute of principle. A substantial yeoman of sense and discernment, will hardly ever be chosen. From these remarks it appears that the government will fall into the hands of the few

---

[304]
http://teachingamericanhistory.org/library/document/objections-to-the-constitution/

175

and the great. This will be a government of oppression. I do not mean to declaim against the great, and charge them indiscriminately with want of principle and honesty.--The same passions and prejudices govern all men. The circumstances in which men are placed in a great measure give a cast to the human character. Those in middling circumstances, have less temptation-- they are inclined by habit and the company with whom they associate, to set bounds to their passions and appetites--if this is not sufficient, the want of means to gratify them will be a restraint--they are obliged to employ their time in their respective callings--hence the substantial yeomanry of the country are more temperate, of better morals and less ambition than the great. The latter do not feel for the poor and middling class; the reasons are obvious--they are not obliged to use the pains and labour to procure property as the other.--They feel not the inconveniences arising from the payment of small sums. The great consider themselves above the common people--entitled to more respect-- do not associate with them--they fancy themselves to have a right of pre-eminence in every thing. In short, they possess the same feelings, and are under the influence of the same motives, as an hereditary nobility. I know the idea that such a distinction exists in this country is ridiculed by some--But I am not the less apprehensive of danger from their influence on this account--Such distinctions exist all the world over--have been taken notice of by all writers on free government--and are founded in the nature of things. It has been the principal care of free governments to guard against the encroachments of the great. Common observation and experience prove the existence of such distinctions. Will any one say, that there does not exist in this country the pride of family, of wealth, of talents; and that they do not command influence and respect among the common people? Congress, in their address to the inhabitants of the province of Quebec, in 1775, state this distinction in the following forcible words quoted from the Marquis Beccaria. "In every human society, there is an essay continually tending to confer on one part the height of power and happiness, and to reduce the other to the extreme of weakness and misery. The intent of good laws is to oppose this effort, and to diffuse their influence universally and equally." We ought to guard against the government being placed in the hands of this class--They cannot have that sympathy with their constituents which is necessary to connect them closely to their interest: Being in the habit of profuse living, they will be profuse in the public expences. They find no difficulty in paying their taxes, and therefore do not feel public burthens: Besides if they govern, they will enjoy the emoluments of the government."[305]

Debates in the various state adopting conventions often centered around the idea that the Constitution would or would not insure the

---

[305] The Founders' Constitution Volume 1, Chapter 13, Document 37 http://press-pubs.uchicago.edu/founders/documents/v1ch13s37.html The University of Chicago Press. Storing, Herbert J., ed. **The Complete Anti-Federalist.** 7 vols. Chicago: University of Chicago Press, 1981.

growth of an aristocracy. Proponents carefully argued that the Constitution was designed to preclude an aristocracy. Arguments were advanced that the condition of our citizenry would not allow for the elevation of an aristocracy, as wealth was fairly evenly divided and because rights of primogeniture and provision for entails had been abolished, thus requiring property to be equally distributed to the children upon death. They had not yet realized that such provisions could be as disastrous to the accumulation of wealth within small social groups as helpful; a realization that had already resulted in methods to defeat these problems over 100 years before.

Charles Pinkney probably summed up one principal argument against the existence of an aristocracy in his speech to the South Carolina Convention on May 14, 1788, saying:

"I am led to conclude, that mediocrity of fortune is a leading feature in our national character, that most of the courses that lead to the destruction of fortune among other nations being removed, and causes of equality existing with us, which are not to be found among then, we may, with safety, assert that the great body of national wealth is nearly equally in the hands of the people, among whom there are a few dangerously rich or a few miserably poor -- that we may congratulate ourselves with living under the blessings of a mild and equal government which knows no distinction but those of merits or talents -- under a government whose honors and offices are equally open to the exertions of all her citizens, and which adopts virtue and worth for her own, wheresoever she can find them."[306]

Unfortunately, for later historians and legal theorists, the major argument was based upon the present popular misconception of the condition of the people. Perhaps it was the acceptance of this present condition argument that led Judge James Wilson to say before the Pennsylvania adoption convention on December 11, 1787, in answer to the argument that the proposed Federal Constitution would establish an aristocracy:

"What particular rights have been reserved to any class of men, or any occasion. Does even the first magistrate of the United States draw to himself a single privilege, or security that does not extend to every person throughout the United States? Is there a single distinction attached to him in this system; more than there is to the lowest offices in the republic? Is there an office from which any one set of men whatsoever are excluded? Is there one of any kind in this system but is as open to the poor as to the rich? To the inhabitant of the country, as well as to the inhabitant of the city?

---

[306] The Debates in the Several State Conventions on the Adoption of The Constitution, Volume 4, p. 323 By James Madison
http://books.google.com/books?id=ccfZAAAAMAAJ&pg=PA323&lpg=PA323&dq=I+am+led+to+conclude,+that+mediocrity+of+fortune+is+a+leading+feature+in+our+national+character&source=bl&ots=Kc_OFR_qLD&sig=gVJz76HnQFaCi3zMunppWfD8fCE&hl=en&sa=X&ei=iRLkU5jjIo_8oATejYKwCA&ved=0CBkQ6AEwAQ#v=onepage&q=I%20am%20led%20to%20conclude%2C%20that%20mediocrity%20of%20fortune%20is%20a%20leading%20feature%20in%20our%20national%20character&f=false

And are these places of honour and emoluments confined to a few? "[307]

Representative Isaac Backus, the elder statesman for and representative of Middleboro, Plymouth County, and a Baptist minister, offered in the Massachusetts Federal Convention on the afternoon of Monday, February 4, 1888, that the Constitution did indeed prohibit accumulation of power, and that this clause was a basic tenet of reserving power to the people in guarding invasion of their other rights or from abuse of their officers of the powers entrusted in them.

"Another great advantage, sir, in the constitution before us, is, its excluding all titles of nobility or hereditary succession of power; which hath been a main engine of tyranny in foreign countries. But the American revolution was built upon the principle, that all men are born with an equal right to liberty and property, and that officers have no right to any power but what is fairly given them by the consent of the people. -- And in the constitution now proposed to us, a power is reserved to the people, constitutionally

[307] **Commentaries on the Constitution of the United States of America:** p 129 By Pennsylvania. Convention, Thomas McKean, James Wilson http://books.google.com/books?id=LaxbAAAAQAAJ&pg=PA129&lpg=PA129 &dq=What+particular+rights+have+been+reserved+to+any+class+of+men,+or+ any+occasion.+Does+even+the+first+magistrate+of+the+United+States+draw+t o+himself+a+single+privilege&source=bl&ots=rYrjkM6MsE&sig=x6IXX6v79 N6JIwms0cwELbjkL_8&hl=en&sa=X&ei=OxXkU8yGLc67oQTy44KYAQ&v ed=0CBQQ6AEwAA#v=onepage&q=What%20particular%20rights%20have% 20been%20reserved%20to%20any%20class%20of%20men%2C%20or%20any %20occasion.%20Does%20even%20the%20first%20magistrate%20of%20the% 20United%20States%20draw%20to%20himself%20a%20single%20privilege&f =false

to reduce every officer again to a private station, and what a guard is this against their invasion of other rights, or abusing of their power? Such a door is now opened, for the establishment of a righteous government, and for securing equal liberty, as never was before opened to any people on earth. "[308]

While Backus thought this proposed government free from aristocracy, Mr. Spencer from Halifax in the North Carolina Federal Convention did not and said that:

"It appears to me, that the powers are too extensive, and not sufficiently guarded. I do not wish that an aristocracy should be instituted. An aristocracy may arise out of this government, though the Members be not hereditary."[309]

Hamilton, the hard-headed realist, while arguing that the proposed Constitution would not set up an aristocracy, admitted other

---

[308] **Commentaries on The Constitution of The United States of America** ...Jonathan Elliot, James Madison, 1866, pp. 150- 151
http://books.google.com/books?id=OS4MAQAAMAAJ&pg=PA150&lpg=PA150&dq=Another+great+advantage,+sir,+in+the+constitution+before+us,+is,+its+excluding+all+titles+of+nobility+or+hereditary+succession+of+power;+which+hath+been+a+main+engine+of+tyranny+in+foreign+countries.&source=bl&ots=FwRWYXCxz5&sig=dX7QIREvflmZ1Hs3IHMSq8DgUMY&hl=en&sa=X&ei=yhfkU6OiHor5oATnvIHwDA&ved=0CBQQ6AEwAA#v=onepage&q=Another%20great%20advantage%2C%20sir%2C%20in%20the%20constitution%20before%20us%2C%20is%2C%20its%20excluding%20all%20titles%20of%20nobility%20or%20hereditary%20succession%20of%20power%3B%20which%20hath%20been%20a%20main%20engine%20of%20tyranny%20in%20foreign%20countries.&f=false

[309] http://docsouth.unc.edu/nc/conv1788/conv1788.xml

circumstances would enable the result. Speaking to the New York Federal Convention, he said:

> "While property continues to be pretty equally divided and a considerable share of information pervades the community, the tendency of the people's suffrages, will be to elevate merit even from obscurity -- as riches increase and accumulate in a few hands; -- as luxury prevails in society, virtue will be in a greater degree considered as only a graceful appendage of wealth, and the tendency of things will be to depart from the republican standard. This is the real disposition of human nature: it is what, neither the honorable member nor myself can correct -- it is a common misfortune, that awaits our state constitution as well as all others."[310]

Though Hamilton could at least be gracious enough to recognize the theoretical class problems raised by representative M. Smith; Mr. Chancellor Livingston would not put up with such notion. With a typical bravado argument of the time, he disposed of such arguments. Discussing the relative opportunities open to rich and poor, the anti-Federalist had noted the rich would succeed. Livingston in rebuttal:

---

[310] **The Founders' Constitution**, Volume 1, Chapter 13, Document 38
http://press-pubs.uchicago.edu/founders/documents/v1ch13s38.html
The University of Chicago Press. *The Papers of Alexander Hamilton*. Edited by Harold C. Syrett et al. 26 vols. New York and London: Columbia University Press, 1961--79

"But, says the gentlemen, the rich will be always brought forward: they will exclusively enjoy the suffrages of the people. For my own part, I believe that if two men of equal abilities set out together in life, one rich, the other of small fortune, the latter will generally take the lead in your government.... "

"The gentleman, sensible of the weakness of this reasoning is obliged to fortify it by having recourse to the phantom aristocracy. I have heard much of this. I always considered it as the bugbear of the party. We are told, that in every country, there is a natural aristocracy, and that this aristocracy consists of the rich and the great: nay, the gentleman goes further, and ranks in this class of men, the wise, the learned, and those eminent for their talents or great virtues. Does a man possess the confidence of his fellow citizens for having done them important services? He is an aristocrat. Has he great integrity? Such a man will be greatly trusted; he is an aristocrat. Indeed, to determine that one is an aristocrat, we need only be assured that he is a man of merit. But I hope we have many such. I hope, sir, we are all aristocrats.... The truth is in these republican governments we know no such ideal distinctions. We are all equally aristocrats. Offices, emoluments, honors are open to all."[311]

---

[311] **The Debates in the Several State Conventions on the Adoption of ...,** Volume 2 By Jonathan Elliot, pp. 269-270.
http://books.google.com/books?id=EjEMAQAAMAAJ&pg=PA269&lpg=PA269&dq=But,+says+the+gentlemen,+the+rich+will+be+always+brought+forward:+they+will+exclusively+enjoy+the+suffrages+of+the+people.&source=bl&ots=JEXhDp30xq&sig=GdHfD9zGW3Cec1zz5RABz3wIPL4&hl=en&sa=X&ei=-S

Governor Morris, hard-headed as Hamilton, had already recognized in the Federal Convention of July 6, 1787, that, in his opinion, reported as:

As to the alarm sounded, of an aristocracy, his creed was that there never was, nor ever will be a civilized Society without an Aristocracy. His endeavor was to keep it as much as possible from doing mischief."[312]

We should note at this point, that these revolutionaries were not thinking of aristocracy in a formal name sense, but rather in the sense of the privileges and powers a few might exercise as against the whole.

From Maryland "A Farmer and Planter" clearly saw the new constitution as establishing an aristocracy. His editorial appearing in the April 1, 1788 issue of the Maryland Journal and Baltimore Advertiser warned:

"The time is nearly at hand, when you are called upon to render up that glorious liberty you obtained, by resisting the tyranny and oppression of George the Third, King of England, and his ministers.... Let me entreat you, my fellows, to consider it well before you act. I have done so, and can find that we are to receive but little good, and a great deal of evil. Aristocracy, or

---

DkU_DJC86BogSM6IHoCg&ved=0CBQQ6AEwAA#v=onepage&q=But%2C%20says%20the%20gentlemen%2C%20the%20rich%20will%20be%20always%20brought%20forward%3A%20they%20will%20exclusively%20enjoy%20the%20suffrages%20of%20the%20people.&f=false

[312] **The Records of the Federal Convention of 1787 [Farrand's Records, Volume 1]** Madison, Friday July 6th. in Convention, p. 545

government in the hands of a very few nobles, or RICH MEN is therein concealed in the most artful wrote plan that ever was formed to entrap a free people."[313]

Should doubters persist who question the existence of the fear of aristocracy at the time, they should now acknowledge that such a fear did exist as a political tool. In Philadelphia, "Montezuma" argued in the October 29, 1787 issue of the Independent Gazetteer:

"Now we the low born, that is, all the people of the United States, except 600 thereabouts, well born, do by this our humble address, declare and most solemnly engage, that we will allow and admit the said 600 well born, immediately to establish and confirm this most noble, most excellent and truly divine constitution. And we further declare that without any equivocation or mental reservation whatever we will support and maintain the same according to the best of our power, and after the manner and custom of all other slaves in foreign countries, namely by the sweat and toil of our body. Nor will we at any future period of time ever attempt to complain of this our royal government, let the consequences be what they may. "[314]

---

[313] The Antifederalist Papers No. 26 *The Use of Coercion by the New Government* (Part I), p. 78

[314] **The Antifederalist Papers No. 27** *The Use of Coercion By the New Government* (Part 2), p. 81

Even the introduction of the restrictions against nobility, (which Richard Henry Lee noted was done "from very great caution"[315] did not go far enough for some accepting states. Both Massachusetts and New Hampshire in their conventions recommended further amending the new proposed constitution to further restrict the acceptance of emoluments from foreign jurisdictions.

Whatever may have been the secret desires of some members of the Constitutional Convention in 1787 for the establishment of an Aristocracy, they were publically disavowed by the proposed Constitution itself in Article I, Sections 9 and 10.

> Article I, Section 9: "No Title of Nobility shall be granted by the United States: and no Person holding any office of Profit or Trust under them, shall, without the consent of the Congress, accept of any present, emolument, Office, or Title, of any kind whatever, from any King, Prince, or foreign state.

---

[315] **Letters From The Federal Farmer** Richard Henry Lee, *Letter XVI* (January 20, 1788) ed. Forrest McDonald (Indianapolis: Liberty Fund 1999). Accessed from http://oll.libertyfund.org/title/690/102320 on 2009-05-22 "Why then by a negative clause, restrain congress from doing what it would have no power to do? This clause, then, must have no meaning, *or imply, that were it omitted, congress would have the power in question, either upon the principle that some general words in the constitution may be so construed as to give it, or on the principle that congress possesses the powers not expressly reserved.* But this clause was in the confederation, and is said to be introduced into the constitution from very great caution. Even a cautionary provision implies a doubt, at least, that it is necessary; and if so in this case, clearly it is also alike necessary in all similar ones."

Article I - Section 10 Clause 1: No State shall .... grant any Title of Nobility.

And so James Madison could write in the Federalist 39 in support of the new Constitution:

> "Could any further proof be required of the republican complexion of this system, the most decisive one might be found in its absolute prohibition of titles of nobility, both under federal and state governments, and in its express guarantee of the republican form of government to each of the latter."[316]

---

[316] **The Federalist Papers.** Oliver H. G. Leigh, Ed. 1901, Universal Classics Library, Vol. II, p. 259.

CHAPTER VII

NOBILITY IN CASE LAW AND LEGAL AUTHORITY

We are told that the nobility clauses have not provided the controlling authority in any "significant" litigation.[317] We should add the caveat "yet."

All words in the Constitution are meaningful. Quoting <u>Holmes v. Jennison</u>,[318]

"Every word appears to have been weighed with the utmost deliberation, and its force and effect to have been fully understood. No word in the instrument, therefore, can be rejected as superfluous or unmeaning..." [319]

Some Congressman must have recalled these restrictions in 1906, because they found their way into the McCarron Act.[320] requiring that applicants for citizenship renounce any titles of nobility.(56) This gave rise to one of the very few judicial interpretations of what is meant by titles of nobility. In <u>Society Vincole Dc. Champagne v. Mumm</u> (CCA 2, 1944)[321] the Second Circuit Court of Appeals made these observations:

---

[317] 16 Am. Jur. 2d, Const. Law 283 n.25 (1997)

[318] <u>Holmes v. Jennison</u>, (1840) 14 Pet. 540, 570- 571, 39 U.S. 540, 568, 10 L.Ed. 579

[319] See also <u>Richfield Oil v. State Board,</u> (1946) 329 U.S. 69 (1946) 77-78, 67 S.Ct. 156. 91 L.Ed. 80

[320] Naturalization Act 1906

[321] <u>Society Vincole Dc. Champagne v. Mumm</u> (CCA 2, 1944) 143 F. 2d 240, 62 QSPQ 2,

"It does not mean abandonment of the name by which an alien has been known. To renounce 'Title' or the 'Order', it can scarcely be necessary always to renounce the name which went with it. "

There is not much case authority on the Nobility clauses Apparently one civil court judge in New York never saw this authority. Judge Maurice Wahl of the Civil Court of New York City rendered two judgments that he appeared to rest on these clauses. They are: Application of Jama, (1966) and Application of Green, (1967).[322] The nobility restriction is mentioned in the first case only, though the second case refers to the first. The court refused to allow Jama to change his name to Von Jama because the judge reasoned that this was adopting a foreign prefix coming from Austria and Germany often denoting nobility. Green was not allowed to adopt a name typically associated with Black Muslims under the reasoning such was un-American and Green was a fine old American name. The Judge became a little confused in citing Art. 1 sec. 9(8) (the federal restriction) in the Jama case, when the least he could have done was cite the state restriction (Art. 1 sec. 10) as the name change was state action. But at least he was aware that there were constitutional restrictions.

Some recent notes in federal cases indicate that the courts may be ready to consider the nobility clauses more seriously as potential

---

[322] Application of Jama, (1966) 272 NYS2d 677, 51 Misc. 2d 9 and Application of Green, (1967) 283 NYS 2d 242, 54 Misc. 2d 607

precedents for future decisions. In <u>Mathews v. Lucas</u>, (1976)[323] Mr. Justice Stevens, joined by Mr. Justice Brennan and Mr. Justice Marshall in dissenting observed in Note 3

"Distinctions between citizens solely because of their ancestry are, by their very nature, odious to a free people whose institutions are founded upon the doctrine of equality. <u>Hirabayashi v. United States</u>, 320 U.S. 81 100. From its inception, the Federal Government has been directed to treat all its citizens as having been "created equal" in the eyes of the law. The Declaration of Independence states:

"We hold these truths to be self-evident, that all men are created equal, that they are endowed by their Creator with certain unalienable Rights, that among these are Life, Liberty and the pursuit of Happiness.

"And the rationale behind the prohibition against the grant of any title of nobility by the United States, *see* U.S.Const., Art. I, § 9, cl. 8, equally would prohibit the United States from attaching any badge of ignobility to a citizen at birth."

Later in <u>Fullilove v. Klutznick</u>, (1980)[324] Mr. Justice Stewart joined by Mr. Justice Rehnquist in their dissent observed:

---

[323] <u>Mathews v. Lucas</u>, (1976) 427 U.S. 495, 516, 520 (n. 3) 96 S.Ct. 1457, 47 L.Ed.2d 731

[324] <u>Fullilove v. Klutznick</u>, (1980) 448 U.S. 448, 531 (n 4/13), 100 S.Ct. 2758. 65 L.Ed.2d 902

"The Fourteenth Amendment was adopted to ensure that every person must be treated equally by each State, regardless of the color of his skin. The Amendment promised to carry to its necessary conclusion a fundamental principle upon which this Nation had been founded -- that the law would honor no preference based on lineage. 4/13

> [Footnote 4/13 The Framers of our Constitution lived at a time when the Old World still tolerated in the shadow of ancient feudal traditions. As products of the Age of Enlightenment, they set out to establish a society that recognized no distinctions among white men on account of their birth. *See* U.S.Const., Art. I, § 9, cl. 8 ("No Title of Nobility shall be granted by the United States"). The words Thomas Jefferson wrote in 1776 in the Declaration of Independence, however, contained the seeds of a far broader principle: "We hold these truths to be self-evident: that all men are created equal. . . ."

Two years later in Zobel v. Williams, (1982)[325] Mr Justice Brennan, in filing a concurring opinion, in which Marshall, Blackmun, and Powell, JJ., joined , supporting the majority opinion that the Federal Government could not follow the Alaska law of in setting aside Alaskan ranking of citizens on the basis of their length of residency, for state privileges, observed:

---

[325] Zobel v. Williams, (1982) 457 U.S. 55, 69 n.3, 102 S.Ct. 2309. 72 L.Ed.2d 672

"But it is significant that the Citizenship Clause of the Fourteenth Amendment expressly equates citizenship only with simple residence. That Clause does not provide for, and does not allow for, degrees of citizenship based on length of residence.[3] And the Equal Protection Clause would not tolerate such distinctions. In short, as much as the right to travel, equality of citizenship is of the essence in our Republic. As the Court notes, States may not "divide citizens into expanding numbers of permanent classes." ....

3. The American aversion to aristocracy developed long before the Fourteenth Amendment and is, of course, reflected elsewhere in the Constitution. See Art. I, § 9, cl. 8 ("No Title of Nobility shall be granted by the United States"). See also Virginia Declaration of Rights (1776), in R. Rutland, The Birth of the Bill of Rights, App. A (1955) ("no man, or set of men, are entitled to exclusive or separate emoluments or privileges from the community, but in consideration of publick services").

At the Circuit Court level in Eskra v. Morton, (7th Cir. 1975)[326] the court reversed the trial court's application of Wisconsin law denying illegitimate native American children inheritances administered by the Federal government and it was observed in the concurring opinion:

---

[326] Eskra v. Morton, (7th Cir. 1975) 524 F.2d 9, 13 n.8.

"If we accepted that premise, and if we thought the discrimination against illegitimates was no different from discrimination in favor of descendants as opposed to ascendants, for example, the mere fact that the government must make Some choice among different potential claimants to intestate property might well be sufficient to justify almost any choice, even one made at random. But plaintiff's interest is not simply economic. Plaintiff has a separate, identifiable interest in not being treated by her government as a second-class person. In our judgment that separate interest is entitled to federal recognition and protection.

The United States, as well as each of the several States, must accord every person within its jurisdiction the equal protection of the laws. Bolling v. Sharpe, 347 U.S. 497, 499, 74 S.Ct. 693, 98 L.Ed. 884; Jimenez v. Weinberger, 417 U.S. 628, 637, 94 S.Ct. 2496, 41 L.Ed.2d 363. From its inception, the Federal Government has been directed to treat all its citizens as having been "created equal" in the eyes of the law.[8]

> n. 8 "We hold these truths to be self-evident, that all men are created equal, that they are endowed by their Creator with certain unalienable Rights, that among these are Life, Liberty and the pursuit of Happiness." The Declaration of Independence.

> The rationale behind the prohibition against the grant of any title of nobility by the United States, see U.S.Const.

art. I, § 9, clause 8, equally would prohibit the United States from attaching any badge of ignobility to a citizen at birth.

Early in our history at least one other court recognized we are dealing with something more than a moniker. The majority of the Supreme Court of Alabama while considering similar restrictions under the Alabama Constitution, in an opinion of Mr .Justice Benjamin Saffold, held in Horst v. Moses,(1872):[327]

> To confer a title of nobility, is to nominate to an order of persons to whom privileges are granted at the expense of the rest of the people. It is not necessarily hereditary, and the objection to it arises more from the privileges supposed to be attached, than to the otherwise empty title or order. These components are forbidden separately in the terms "privilege", "honor'", and "emolument", as they are collectively in the term "title of nobility". The prohibition is not affected by any consideration paid or rendered for the grant. Its purpose is to preserve the equality of citizens in respect to their public and private rights.

> "How shall we distinguish these prohibitions from the undoubted right of the State to grant certain franchises to particular individuals in exclusion of others, as a ferry or a corporation, or to contract with its citizens, as for the

---

[327] Horst v. Moses, 48 Ala. 129, 142 (1872), appeal denied 82 U.S. 387, 15 Wal. 387, 21 L.Ed 176, (1872) on subsequent appeal 52 Ala. 198

construction of public works? The theory of our government is the recognition of the utmost liberty of the citizen consistent with the welfare of the society. No restraint imposed by law can find justification elsewhere than in the consideration of the public good. There are necessities and conveniences that can only be supplied to the public by committing the duty or privilege of doing so to a few. One ferry or toll-bridge is sometimes secured only by forbidding two."[328]

The Horst case is possibly the only judicial attempt to ever try to give titles of nobility any real judicial interpretation in deciding a case. The facts reveal that the respondent, Moses, and his friends had a nice gambling operation going on in Mobile, Alabama with a charitable association as a front. All of this activity had been carefully codified by a special act of the Alabama legislature enfranchising the operation. By general law, gambling was illegal in Alabama. Horst and the other Mobile City Fathers sought to close the gamblers and the gamblers applied to the State Courts for temporary and permanent restraining orders. The lower court granted a temporary restraining order which was appealed to the Alabama Supreme Court in 1872.

The Alabama Supreme Court was united on dissolving the temporary restraining order but divided on its reasoning with two justices of three apparently concurring that the Alabama constitution restriction, "no title of nobility, or hereditary distinction, privilege, honor or emolument, shall ever be granted or conferred in this State",

---

[328] Ibid

applied. The third justice felt the word "hereditary" controlled the application of that whole section and thus could not apply and reversed based upon another argument. No hereditary limitation can be found in the federal constitution. Justice Benjamin Saffold,[329] was from Selma, Alabama, and a highly respected legal mind at the time. He sat on the Supreme Court bench from 1868 until 1874. He spoke for the majority on the constitutional points.

Having observed that titles of nobility were neither empty names nor necessarily hereditary, he went on to note that what was forbidden separately in the form of privileges, distinctions, emoluments and honors were doubly forbidden by the term "titles of nobility". Thereupon, he came to the thorny center of the problem. How could the state grant any private franchises, such as for railroads, ferries and toll bridges? This required a fine bit of legal hair-splitting, which he did in this manner:

---

[329] Benjamin Franklin. Saffold, was a son of Reubin Saffold III, former Chief Justice of the Alabama Supreme Court. He was born in 1826, was graduated at Tuscaloosa, read law under his father, and came to the bar in 1847. Settling in Cahaba, he practiced till appointed to the circuit bench by Military Gov. Parsons in 1865. Defeated the following year for this position by Hon. John Moore of Perry, he was appointed mayor of Selma in 1867 by Gen. Swayne, and the same year was a member of the convention called by the military authorities to frame a State constitution. The following year it is reported that he was placed on the bench of the supreme court by an act of congress where he served for six years. Brewer's Alabama History 1540-1872. However he may have been elected, a the new constitution of 1768 provided such choice. This opinion might identify him as a radical reconstructionists filled with the egalitarian spirit of the times that saw the adoption of the 13th, 14th and 15th Amendments to the Constitution. http://www.magnoliabuzz.com/books/brewer/al-county-dallas-saffold2.php and http://saffold.com/history/?p=6 Perhaps worthy of further study.

"Extreme cases sometimes illustrate a principle when intermediate ones serve only to confuse. The right of way for the construction of a railroad is conceded to be a fit subject for the exercise of the State's right of eminent domain, though the recipient is a private party. But a proposition to confer upon the same party the exclusive privilege of selling drugs or liquors would be justly regarded as an outrage. The test of the State's authority, therefore, is this: the privilege that can be conferred must conduce to the public good, and be such as is obliged to be committed to a few in order to be available. "[330]

The court goes on to examine the nature of corporations in general as affected by this test. In distinguishing the private, as opposed to the public "municipal" or governmental corporation, the court gives this interesting reasoning for general incorporations acts:

"In further proof of this test, the power of the legislature to charter corporations, not municipal, heretofore not questioned, has been specially granted by the constitution, and restricted to the passage of general laws from the benefits of which none are excluded who may comply with the conditions prescribed. Const. Art. 13, § 1. This change of the fundamental law was doubtless due to the conviction that the prohibition against exclusive privileges had not been sufficiently observed by the legislature and the courts."[331]

---

[330] 48 Ala @ 144

[331] 48 Ala @ 143

The court then comes to the problem confronted in this case; the general public is excluded from the right to gamble while Moses and friends are granted the privilege. The court found that gambling is a right that is subject to legislative prohibition. It is subject to "Mala prohibita", which may be understood as those matters which, though they are not bad in and of themselves, are of such indifferent nature that they may yet be prohibited by the legislative body, like most traffic laws today. Gambling appears to have been such a subject in the mind of the court. Thus, the court is faced with balancing of rights in the framework of equality of personal freedom.

> "Experience has since shown a necessity for controlling somewhat the discretion of the legislature in the interest of freedom of personal action; and hence come the rights 'reserved to the people'. To prohibit the pursuit of- necessary business, or to commit it to a few, to the exclusion of the rest of the people, would be a flagrant usurpation on the part of the legislature. Setting up a lottery is conceded to be the subject of the mala prohibita. Therefore, either the act in question confers an unconstitutional privilege, or the law prohibiting the people generally from setting up lotteries withholds a constitutional or reserved right. There is no doubt about which must fall."[332]

The dissent of .Justice Peters is interesting as he heavily relies upon the word "hereditary" that appears in the Alabama Constitution and

---

[332] 48 Ala @ 145

is, of interest here, absent from the clauses under consideration in the Federal Constitution.

It is also patent to my mind that the general assembly has power to make such a grant, and that this power is not intended to be interfered with, by the thirty-second section of the first article of the State constitution. The mere recital of this section of our fundamental law, without more, would seem to refute this idea. I quote its words, so far as they apply to this case. They are these: No title of nobility, or hereditary distinction, privilege, honor, or emolument, shall ever be granted or conferred in this State. - Const. Ala. Art. I, § 32. These words scarcely need interpretation to find out their true sense; that is, the sense in which they were used by the people in their highest State law. Obviously, the people intended, by these words, to impose some limitation on the legislative will of the general assembly. But they did not intend to go beyond what had formerly been customary. They did not intend to cut off the power to grant, for limited periods, merited distinctions and honors to the citizens who had rendered great and important services to the State, or to grant privileges or emoluments to be used for the public good. In other words, they did not intend to. prohibit all right to grant any privilege, franchise or emolument whatever. Had this been their purpose, the language used would have been without any qualifying and limiting adjective. The word 'hereditary' would have been left out of the sentence altogether. This word qualifies the whole series of particulars enumerated in the sentence, as if it had been repeated before each. The State constitution of 1819 contains a section of similar import with that above quoted, and almost in the identical words. Yet many franchises and exclusive privileges were granted under it, without objection -- such as the right to establish toll-bridges, toll- causeways, ferries, and the supplying cities with pure water and gas-lights. Const. Ala. 1819, Art. 1, 26; Clay's Dig. p. 27; Code of Ala. p. 31; Revised Code, Rg 1383, 1389; Mobile Water [* 148] Works, Montgomery Gas *Works; and see the discussions in Dale v. Governor, 3 Stew. 387; Stein v. Mayor of Mobile. 17 Ala. 234, S.C. 24 Ala. 591; People v. Utica Ins. Co., 15 Johns, 358 [8 Am. Dec. 243]; Presit, &c., of Newbury and Cochecton Turnpike Road v. Miller, 5 Johns, Ch. 101 [9 Am. Dec. 274]; Micou v. Tallassee Br. Co., January term, 1871 [47 Ala. 652]. The power to grant and confer privileges, honors or emoluments, intended to be prohibited, were such as were 'hereditary', and not such as were limited to a reasonable length of time."[333]

We include this long quote from Justice Peters to make it clear that the court was not necessarily divided on the meaning of the Titles of Nobility restriction. They only disagreed on the application of that clause. It is submitted that the Titles of Nobility clause in the Federal Constitution has as much or more potential influence on the future of

---

[333] 48 Ala @ 147

America as the fourteenth Amendment ever had. It is a fascinatingly legal precedent in gestation that may yet require a Caesarian birth.

The Horst case was appealed to the United States Supreme Court which dismissed the appeal as it was not from a final judgment.[334] On the second appeal to the Alabama Supreme Court after final judgment in the lower court, the Alabama Supreme Court again reviewed the lower court but Justice Saffold was no longer on the bench. The court confirmed its earlier ruling but only used the second constitutional argument, that the bill did not purport to implement its title and made no further mention of titles of nobility.[335] As the later ruling did not overrule or repudiate the earlier opinion of Justice Saffold, it could still be considered good law in the State of Alabama. I have found no published constitutional scholar who has ever discussed it.

The legal reasoning in this amazing case illustrates the revolutionary proportions of the clause. It goes much further than saying that all persons shall have the equal protection of the laws. It attacks any legal structure that allows inequality of circumstances which depend upon the structure of the laws. It was not something that came out of the 1917 Russian revolution, the Chinese revolution, or even the French revolution. It came out of the true Atlantic Revolutionary spirit of the American revolution actually predating independence and was born contemporaneously with and almost simultaneously with our Declaration of Independence, between June 11 and July 12, 1776. Similar

---

[334] 82 U.S. 387, 15 Wal. 387, 21 L.Ed 176, (1872)

[335] Moses Beebe v. Mayor etc. of Mobile, (1875) 52 Ala, 198

restrictions, though closer to the breadth of the restriction in the *Agreement of the Free People of England*, were embodied in the Preamble and Title I of the French Constitution of 1791.

When it is understood that since 1893 in interpreting the Chinese Exclusion Act of May 5, 1892, the Federal Government has consistently held that the fundamentals of the equal protection clause have no application to Federal law by virtue of the Fifth Amendment, Article 1 s 9(8) takes on tremendous importance. In re Sing Lee(1893).[336] Could opinions of the Supreme Court condoning unequal Federal tax treatment as in Helvering v. Lerner Stores, Co. (1941),[337] or unequal treatment in commerce in the case of Sunshine Anthracite Coal Co. v. Adkins, (1940)[338] be reversed by this new revolutionary approach? The Supreme Court was not wrong under any literal reading of the Fifth Amendment, but what of the equality demanded by the Titles of Nobility restrictions on the actions of the federal government requiring our classless society?

The United States Supreme Court has not defined the subject. All one will find in the cases is the dicta mentioned before and

---

[336] In re Sing Lee(1893); 54 Fed. 334, 337.

[337] Helvering v. Lerner Stores, Co. (1941), 314 U.S. 463, 62 S. Ct. 341, 86 L. Ed. 343,

[338] Sunshine Anthracite Coal Co. v. Adkins, (1940) 310 U.S. 381, 84 L. Ed. 1263, 60 S. Ct. 407

comments mentioning the restrictions in dicta as this from the case of Downes v. Bidwell, (1901)[339]:

> "There is a clear distinction between such prohibitions as go to the very root of the power of Congress to act at all, irrespective of the time or place, and such as are operative on 'throughout the United States', or among the several States.

> "Thus, when the constitution declares that 'no bill of attainder or ex post facto law shall be passed' and that 'no title of nobility shall be granted by the United States', it goes to the competency of Congress to pass a bill of that description. " (See also Julliard v. Greenman (1884), 110 U.S. 421, (4 S. Ct. 122, 28 Ed. 204.)

One would hope that if lawyers ever get around to drafting a complaint based upon the federal nobility restriction, they will remember it applies to "the United States" and not merely to the competency of Congress despite what the Supreme Court has said in dicta and Lee said in argument. In other words, even the Supreme Court, other courts or the President and executive branch alone or in combination with Congress. could do the granting were it not prohibited.

From the very thin line of case authority we might, guardedly, conclude that the restrictions on granting titles of nobility refer to something more than names, perhaps special privileges, powers,

---

[339] Downes v. Bidwell, (1901) 182 U.S. 244, 277, 45 L. Ed. 1088, 1102, 21 S. Ct. 770:

distinctions, places, emoluments and pensions and that dependency of these privileges, powers, places, distinctions, emoluments and pensions upon hereditary devolution is not necessary for them to be unconstitutional if granted or protected by governmental action.

The constitutional treatises of legal scholars Cooley and Crosskey offer little assistance.[340] However, Justice Story gives these restrictions remarkable powers. One would have thought that he had taken Hamilton seriously.

> This clause seems scarcely to require even a passing notice, As a perfect equality is the basis of all our institutions, state and national, the prohibition against the creation of any title of nobility seems proper, if not indispensable, to keep perpetually alive a just sense of this important truth. Distinction between citizens in regard to rank would soon lay the foundation of odious claims and privileges, and silently subvert the spirit of independence and personal dignity, which are so

---

[340] William Winslow Crosskey: **Politics and the Constitution** (1955 ed) especially 1: p. 421. Thomas M. Cooley: **Constitutional Limitations** (6th ed. 1890) especially p. 28. Nor is Edward S. Corwin much help: see **The Constitution of the United States of America, Analysis and Interpretation** (1952) especially p. 374. Also of no use James Dewitt Andrews: **American Law. A Commentary on the Jurisprudence, Constitution and Laws of the United States** (2 ed 1908) Vol I §463 p. 586, Cass R. Sunstein, *The Anticaste Principle,* MICH. L. REV. 2410, 2428-29 (1994) (arguing that the Nobility Clauses originate in anti-caste principles).

often proclaimed to be the best security of a republican government,"[341]

Joel Tiffany reaches similar conclusions when he says:

"(T)he general government has no authority to create classes or class distinctions among the people; - that all its laws shall be enacted upon the hypothesis that all men are created equal, and are equally entitled at the hands of their government; - that government is an institution of the people, created for the sole and only purpose of administering their authority, to the end that each and all may be secure in the enjoyment of civil liberty: and that <u>equal</u> and exact justice may be administered to all; ... "[342]

If those be the purposes of these clauses, then one has some difficulty with the reason for adoption of the equal protection clause in the' Fourteenth Amendment. Some have thought that clause might have been adopted to include corporations under equal protection of the laws along with natural persons. Perhaps its adoption has avoided application of equal protection of the laws to federal acts as the Fourteenth Amendment only applies to the states. Or perhaps by the end of the Civil War such social stratifications existed that the amendment was adopted to emphasize some minimum equality of protection in the laws rather than to provide some limitation of

---

[341] Joseph Story: **Commentaries on the Constitution of the United States,** (5th Ed. 1891) sec. 1351.

[342] Joel Tiffany: **A Treatise on Government and Constitutional Law** (1863) sec. 476 p. 297.

privilege to be raised as a basis for equality. Such an approach is more conducive to logical legal reasoning especially considering the normal legal rights lawyers were then obliged to protect.

Modern scholars also consider a broader approach. Professor J.L. Balkin wrote that the concern was with much more than mere conferral of titles. The concern was with the entire social system of superiority and inferiority, of habits of deference and condescension, of social rank and political, cultural and economic privilege.[343]

Carlton F.W. Larson has suggested that constitutional history argues that the Framers intended the clauses to forbid not only the actual titles of nobility, but also governmental creation of elite classes with unequal material advantages and privileged political access.");[344]

We have seen from the vast social application of the equal protection clause that when we start defining our constitutional provisions in these broad terms and applying them with the force of law, we have a social revolution on our hands. Of course, some might comment that such is the origin of the restrictions. Yet state action has been so broadly defined that this writer pales before adopting such a Mao little Red Book late 20th Century Chinese approach of continual

---

[343] J.M. Balkin, *The Constitution of Status*, 106 YALE L.J. 2313, 2350 (1996) (citing Gordon S. Wood, **The Radicalism of the American Revolution** (1992) pp. 41-42

[344] Carlton F.W. Larson, *Titles of Nobility, Hereditary Privilege, and the Unconstitutionality of Legacy Preferences in Public School Admissions*, 4 WASH. U. L.R. 1375, 1381, 1401-02, 1408 (2006)

revolution to our society. Caution, nevertheless, dictates that we would be foolish to overlook the potential revolutionary implications in these constitutional restrictions. They embodied the bases of the eighteenth century revolutionary ideas of equality in society into our constitution, our basic law. We are still discovering where those ideas go and what they mean..

The foolhardy might say that these clauses could never be used in the manner suggested by Story, Tiffany or the proposed Constitution of 1649. Our Supreme Court has taught us the folly of such complacency. The great legal scholar, Oliver Wendell Holmes warns us:

> But the provisions of the Constitution are not mathematical formulas having their essence in their form; they are organic, living institutions. They [sic] significance is vital, not formal; it is gathered not simply by taking a dictionary, but by considering their origin and the line of their growth."[345]

There is no safety in observing that the development of our nation has not been towards forms of then existing nobility or aristocracy. Justice Stone observed:[346]

> :"But in determining whether a provision of the Constitution applies to a new subject matter, it is of little significance that it

---

[345] See Gompers v. United States, (1913) 233 U.S. 604, 21 L.Ed. 1115, 34 S.Ct. 693.

[346] United States v. Classic, (1940) 313 U.S. 299. 315, 85 L.Ed. 1368, 1378, 61 S.Ct. 1031. Rehearing denied 314 U.S. 707,, 86 L.Ed. 565, 62 S.Ct. 51.

is one with which the framers were not familiar, for in setting up an enduring framework of government they undertook to carry out for the indefinite future and in all vicissitudes of the changing affairs of men, those fundamental purposes which the instrument itself discloses. Hence we read its words, not as we read legislative codes which are subject to continuous revision with the changing course of events, but as the revelation of the great purposes which were intended to be achieved by the Constitution as a continuing instrument of government. [Cases cited]

"If we remember 'it is a Constitution we are expounding' we cannot rightly prefer, of the possible meaning of its words, that which will defeat rather than effectuate the constitutional purpose.

"To decide it we turn to the words of the Constitution read in their historical setting as revealing the purposes of its framers, and in search for admissible meanings of its words which, in the circumstances of their application will effectuate those purposes."

Implied therein is examination of more than the original. historical context of the words. Justice Holmes brings this out in an opinion of 1919:[347]

---

[347] Missouri v. Holland (1919) 252 U.S. 416, 64 L.Ed. 641, 40 S.Ct. 382, 11 ALR 984

"...(W)hen we are dealing with the words that also area constituent act, like the Constitution of the United States, we must realize that they have called into life a being the development of which could not have been foreseen completely by the most gifted of its begetters. It was enough for them to realize or to hope that they had created an organism; it has taken a century and cost their successors much sweat and blood to prove that they created a nation. The case before us must be considered in the light of our whole experience, and not merely in that of what was said a hundred years ago. "

Taking our whole experience, we encounter the basic problem with restraints upon privilege. One person's privilege is another's property. The freedom of speech of one may deny the freedom of speech of others. Nothing emphasizes this more than the passage of time. It is the passage of time within the social continuum free from disruptive forces that enhances privilege and diminishes freedom. Jefferson saw this and attempted to formulate some practical theory for overcoming the problem. He sought, as did the Levelers, in the Constitutional Proposal of 1649, and many revolutionaries since, to abolish privilege while retaining some advantage of private property. Thomas Jefferson wrote to James Madison. 6 Sept. 1789:

The course of reflection in which we are immersed here on the elementary principles of society has presented this question to my mind; and that no such obligation can be so transmitted I think very capable of proof.--I set out on this ground, which I suppose to be self evident, *"that the earth belongs in usufruct to the living"*: that the dead have neither powers nor rights over it. The portion occupied by an individual ceases to be his when himself ceases to be, and reverts to the society. If the society has formed no rules for the appropriation of it's lands in severality, it will be taken by the first occupants.[348]

This principle that the earth belongs to the living, and not to the dead, is of very extensive application and consequences, in every country, and most especially in France. It enters into the resolution of the questions Whether the nation may change the descent of lands holden in tail? Whether they may change the appropriation of lands given anciently to the church, to hospitals, colleges, orders of chivalry, and otherwise in perpetuity? Whether they may abolish the charges and privileges attached on lands, including the whole catalogue ecclesiastical and feudal? It goes to hereditary offices, authorities and jurisdictions; to hereditary orders, distinctions and appellations; to perpetual monopolies in commerce, the arts and sciences; with a long train of et ceteras:[349]

---

[348] The Papers of Thomas Jefferson. Edited by Julian P. Boyd et al. Princeton: Princeton University Press, 1950 15:392--97

[349] Ibid.

We further note, that these are very environmentally friendly concepts denying anyone the right to cause permanent injury to the earth as they cannot claim ownership to do so. They are taking the properties of future generations.

"The Earth belongs to the living, not to the dead. The will and the power of man expire with his life, by nature's law. Some societies give it an artificial continuance, for the encouragement of industry; some refuse it, as our aboriginal neighbors, whom we call barbarians. The generations of men may be considered as bodies or corporations. Each generation has the usufruct of the earth during the period of its continuance. When it ceases to exist, the usufruct passes on to the succeeding generation, free and unencumbered, and so on; successively, from one generation to another forever.[350]

We may consider each generation as a distinct nation, with a right, by the will of its majority, to bind themselves, but none to bind the succeeding generation, more than the inhabitants of another country. Or the case may be likened to the ordinary one of a tenant for life, who may hypothecate the land for his debts, during the continuance of his usufruct; but

[350] *Thomas Jefferson to John Wayles Eppes, 1813.* Saul K. Padover, ed. **Thomas Jefferson on Democracy** (13th Printing) pp 15, 16. See also Memorial Edition, Ford Edition 13:169, http://famguardian.org/Subjects/Politics/ThomasJefferson/jeff1340.htm

at his death, the reversioner (who is also for life only) receives it exonerated from all burthen (sic). "[351]

Jefferson saw the problem with this arrangement. Usufruct, a civil law word not in the common law tradition, means the right, or privilege of use of a thing, such as a farm, and enjoying its rents and profits, but without wasting the thing itself. He considered them more as life estates in property, but with a duty to maintain it for the next generation or people. Considering the problem from an agrarian background, he considered it might be possible to set up arbitrary time periods over which laws, social contracts might be effective. He turned to mortality tables for his formula and found that generations then came and went on an average of nineteen years.

From his statement we may presume that he had some inkling that life estates in objects can be a limitation on industry from their own limitation of individual expectancy. What is not recognized is that society can base its cohesive forces on theories accepting waste (or could before our modern ecologists took the floor). Jefferson was very intense about restricting the dead hand. In 1823 he wrote:

"That our Creator made the earth for the use of the living and not the dead; that those who exist not can have no use nor right in it, no authority or power over it; that one generation of men cannot foreclose or burthen (sic) its use to another,

---

[351] *Thomas Jefferson To: John W. Eppes, June 24, 1813,*
http://illinoisconservative.com/Jefferson/tj-public-debt-1.html

which comes to it in its own right and by the same divine beneficence; that a preceding generation cannot bind a succeeding one by its laws or contracts; these deriving their obligation from the will of the existing majority, and that majority being removed by death, another comes in its place with a will equally free to make its own laws and contracts; these are axioms so self- evident that no explanation can make them plainer." [352]

Obviously generations do not come and go in some convenient fashion allowing any one generation freedom from its former or its successor. Death is not so convenient. Even as the animate participants die, their contemporaries, their inanimate possessions, abstract ideas and influence survive them. We no longer bury our members' wealth with their bodies. To increase the social utility of wealth, we have endowed it with a certain autonomy. This endowment is in itself the major step of transference of objects of wealth from absolute private property, indistinguishable, from the possessor, to something more in the nature of privilege. It is also involved in separating wealth from humans that create and use it, and even permitting some humans to determine what that wealth is actually.

---

[352] ***Thomas Jefferson to Thomas Earle. September 24, 1823***
http://www.yamaguchy.com/library/jefferson/1823.html
The Writings of Thomas Jefferson, editor H.A. Washington New York : H.W. Derby, 1861

Fine distinctions in the terms Private property and privilege are elusive items. As abstract ideas they are best legally analyzed with a socially considered necessary connection of individuals or persons to the control of certain powers over animate or inanimate objects, useful or harmful, in varying degrees, in society. These powers exist by reason of a more general human confidence that their existence may be utilized for some purpose or purposes, Where the use may be beneficial, the powers may be called wealth, but are not necessarily so called.

Our society is a continuum of existence and each individual death is a direct threat to it. Death threatens the continuum of control which raises the specter of possible social fratricide because suddenly autonomous items of wealth are free in the community. To a greater or lesser extent bankruptcy, divorce, political and military defeat, revolution and other similar events also threaten to disrupt the continuum of society. But death is the regular occurrence. As its occurrence is regular, but individual prediction is difficult. To insure that our autonomous property does not give us grounds for internal conflict or self-destruction we adopt general laws, socially accepted practices, and forms of contracts to cover the event. It is difficult to fit these laws and contracts within any arbitrary time frame. This was ably recognized by a very good friend and tutor of Mr. Jefferson, and a lesser known member of our founding fathers, George Withe.

Withe had a distinguished career as a member of the Virginia bar. He was a representative to the Virginia legislature and to the Continental Congress. He was Thomas Jefferson's legal tutor and was chosen as the first law professor at William and Mary during Jefferson's term as President of Virginia. He sat for some time as a justice on the High Court of Chancery in Virginia, where he made the following observations in a footnote to a case in 1793. He was selected as a delegate from Virginia to the Constitutional Convention but had to return home early because of sickness in the family. It was suspicioned that his life was cut short by a dose of poison administered by his nephew.

"That laws, of civil institution, derive their obligation from the consent of those, who were members of the community, when the laws were instituted, must be admitted. But, if the obligation ceases with the existence of those individual legislators, which must be the consequence of denying the obligation of the law upon individuals, who did not consent to it, the laws could not be perpetual, as many laws are said to be, nor catholic, as all laws ought to be. Besides, many laws are enacted against the consent of (a) great part of the community.

"The vigor of instituted laws, if it survive the original legislators, must be continued, not by the, consent of succeeding generations, declared individually, but by some other principle: and that is natural reason.

"Without society, mankind, if they could exist and propagate, would be wretched; their native rights would be frequently violated; the enjoyment of acquired rights be precarious; nor could society be preserved without civil institutions and regulations. Hence, the obligation to observe and conform to those institutions and regulations, by the law of nature, devolves upon men, who could not consent to them.

"This doctrine is not derogatory to rational civil liberty, which is to be free from all civil obligation, except such as laws, enacted by consent of society, or representatives of their election, had created; and to be free from those obligations, when the same society, of representatives, shall signify their will to abrogate the laws, which did create the obligations.

"But what is the same society? For no nation, at the end of an hour, consists of those individual men of whom it consisted at the beginning of that period.

"By national identity must be meaned (sic) a mystical union of members by successive generations, whereof one imperceptibly renovates the decay of another, a kind immortality being one of the attributes of a nation,..."[353]

---

[353] E. Page & C. V. Pendleton & C.. 1 Withe 211, 215, 1 VRA 221, 222 (1793) and/or 1 RA 86, et seq. Memoir of Author (1852 ed) Hon. Littleton W. Tarewell and Henry Clay biographers.

Withe is very close to the practical heart of the problem. Society, even revolutionary society, creates a continuous communicative symbolism of itself to insure that minimum cohesion and continuity necessary for avoidance of self-destruction. In our law, these symbolisms have been formed in the corporate or body politic theories of inter-social relations and the provisions for devolution of powers over the animate and inanimate, tangible and intangible objects of social confidence wherever their present executors are disturbed in their possession and execution. This is not said to deny that within any defined society may exist completely divergent and at points antagonistic theories for achieving such results.

Franklin recognized other practical limitations on property with implied thoughts for resolutions, which are worth notice here. In his letter of December 25, 1783 to Robert Morris he expressed it thusly:

> "All the Property that is necessary to a man, for the Conservation of the Individual and the Propagation of the Species, is his natural Right, which none can justly deprive him of: But all Property superfluous to such purposes is the. Property of the Public. "[354]

---

[354] Smyth, Albert Henry, Editor: **The Writings of Benjamin Franklin**. 10 vols. New York: Macmillan Co., 1905--7. Vol 1. Ch 16, Document 12 *Benjamin Franklin letter December 25, 1783 to Robert Morris* http://press-pubs.uchicago.edu/founders/documents/v1ch16s12.html

There is a practical amplification of power of control, the perception of which can only be perceived through necessity and communication thereof. We should continue to bear in mind Hamilton's second observation that diffusion of information aids in diffusion of control. This observation should be as important to those in control at any time as those out of control, because only an approach of total perception of both aid either in understanding their own or the other's position.

CHAPTER VIII

SOME THOUGHTS TOWARDS MEANING

"We should remember that the nobility clauses were adopted because the founders were concerned not only about the bestowal of titles but also about an entire social system of superiority and inferiority, of habits of deference and condescension, of social rank, and political, cultural and economic privilege."[355]

Today, what do these restrictions on titles of nobility mean? There are several points of view which can be reached with some plausible argument. The simplest point of view is that when the revolutionary Continental Congress decided to proscribe nobility, they were thinking of an order of prestige entitled to its own group voice within the government that had to be represented by its own house in the legislative assembly. Hence they made the United Sates Senate an aristocratic institution subject to appointments by the State legislatures. But the 17th Amendment changed that by calling for their direct election by the people of each state, and introducing a modicum of democracy into the Senate, cleverly

---

[355] Gordon S. Wood, <u>The Radicalism of the American Revolution</u> 11-24 (1991)

denied by its rules,[356] in addition to lack of democracy in the nation as a whole because of disparities in State populations.

Of course, the Constitution is not a democratic document but was formed to promote a social order more reflective of the English 18th Century. We pointed out in the *Filibuster Solution*

"The United States is not a democracy. It is an unequal Republic. 25 of the least populous states, half of the United States, contain less that one sixth of the total population of the country.

"The least populous state, Wyoming, has less than .2% of the total population of the United States and its territories. .... Wyoming has two senators. Either one of them can threaten a filibuster and cripple consideration of issues or appointments before the Senate. Even if the Cloture rule were changed to allow 51% of the Senate to approve a cloture, this would still only represent about one sixth of the total population of the United States.[357]

Admittedly there have been some improvement in the Filibuster rules since I wrote this in 2011, by some minor relaxation of the Filibuster rules on certain appointments. They are still largely in effect so that the already aristocratically constructed institution

---

[356] Edward D Campbell, **Filibuster Solution: The People's Answer to The Senate's Super Majority Rules or Returning the Senate to The States and the People** (2011)

[357] **Filibuster Solution**, supra, p. 11

can be enabled to be even more so by the Filibuster rules now further reinforced by the judiciary's more recent allowance of mostly unbridled influences of wealth in selection of members.

Of course, wealth has always been the continuous mark of the power of aristocracy, landed, mercantile, industrial or financial. I pointed out in 2011 how the Filibuster so rigged the system that senators opposing any legislation can block it not only with 41 votes, but can do so with votes having a better than two to one electoral population ratio so they can block the will of the vast majority of the electorate.[358]   It is a very rigged system, which has been further empowered by the gerrymandering of House of Representative's congressional districts.

Should we consider the Nobility clauses only to apply to names? This is definitely too narrow. The Constitution was written at a minimal word expense to be interpreted in the future. None of these words are necessarily narrow in interpretation. The very factor of the double force of the nobility restrictions should emphasize that truth. In England peerage was not confirmed until the person to whom the original letters patent had been issued had actually taken his seat in The House of Lords during an actual session of Parliament. In effect, though the King granted peerage, the House of Lords confirmed it in legislative assembly. But the legislative assembly did not include all of the Nobility.

_____

[358] Supra, p. 3.

The abolition of the Parliamentary House of Lords on March 19, 1649[359] by the House of Commons as a result of the English Civil War did not outlaw or destroy the nobility, (probably because its members participated on both sides and continued to be responsible for some local social stability and local and national economy). While there were discussions of social and economic reforms at the time, none were permanently made. After the decade of interregnum and mostly Cromwellian rule, a new Convention Parliament was called and the temporal Lords resumed their seats in their own house of the Parliament. That Parliament restored the monarchy in the person of Charles II in 1660. The Spiritual Lords of the Church of England who had been barred from participating by legislation during the Long Parliament in 1642,[360] were readmitted by legislation in 1661.[361]

Our forefathers' knowledge of the terms of nobility does not seem to have been restricted to those quaint isles across the Channel from Europe. There were many forms of nobility upon the continent which may or may not have had any formal influence or place within the established state or growing nationalistic governments.

---

[359] Samuel Rawson Gardner, ed..**Constitutional Documents of the Puritan Revolution,** (1906) March 19, 1649. Scobell, ii. 8. See **Commonwealth and Protectorate,** i. 3.

[360] John Raithby, ed. (1819) [1642]. *Charles I, 1640: An Act for disinabling all persons in Holy Orders to exercise any temporall jurisdiccion or authoritie.* Statutes of the Realm. 5 (1628-80)

[361] Clergy Act 1661 (13 Car. II, St. I, c.2)

This writer is inclined to support that position that the term "nobility" signified possession of some forms of governmental influence and/or patronage or preferment but that this was not an exclusive requirement. In this we are indebted to the work of R.R. Palmer; the two volume edition (1959) **The Age of the Democratic Revolution** Note 111.   Palmer traced the various democratic-aristocratic movements throughout the United States and Europe during the American and French Revolutions. One of his more interesting points was that despite the terrible image of the French Revolution, based upon death and immigration in comparable statistics between the two, the American Revolution might be considered a much greater internal revolution. Jackson Turner Main in his study of significant statistical data based on election polls and probate records, among other things, tentatively bears the revolutionary thesis out on the American side of the Atlantic in ***The Social Structure of Revolutionary America*** (1965).[362]

An example of the times can be found in a famous phrase that exists to this day, often attributed to Charles Lynch who held extrajudicial power in his court in Virginia during the Revolutionary war, meeting out summary justice that included whipping, property seizure, coerced pledges of allegiance, and conscription into the military of suspected loyalists. His extra-judicial acts were later legitimized by the Virginia General

---

[362] Jackson Turner Main. **The Social Structure of Revolutionary America**. ... Princeton University Press, 1965

Assembly in 1782, perhaps giving rise to the infamous phrase of "Lynch's Law."[363]

The French, before their revolution, while not only being the most populous of European countries, was also considered one of the most progressive. The literacy rate may have been the highest in Europe. The starvation--deprivation pictured from such novels as a "**Tale of Two Cities**" seems to have been largely overplayed. Probably some just plain stupid politics by the King had as much to do with the reign of terror as any other factor. Furthermore, the natives in Paris did not have the British navy nor its army to contend with that clearly discouraged Americans from any wide blood bath of Tories. These forces would discourage such activities by citizens of the American leading cities: Boston, New York, Charleston, Baltimore, and Philadelphia for example. The French King vacillated between support of the bourgeoisie and the aristocracy and in the end lost any real support he could have rallied from either. Palmer notes that when the national sovereign supported himself with the aristocracy he was generally prevalent in the various European revolutions of the time. They had most of the money and armies have to be paid.

This has underlying significance in governmental theory concerning the source and use of power. This theoretical subject must be studied to develop any idea of the significance then and now of the term "nobility". The King's power was his prerogative,

---

[363] http://en.wikipedia.org/wiki/Charles_Lynch_(jurist)

used by him and those closely connected to whom it was delegated. This had some setback in England in the 1640's and 1688, but under the Georges, through the use of the King's influence, it was definitely regaining de facto status in the English commonwealth of the eighteenth century. George III seizure of the western lands is a clear statement of that power.

Today, as then, the power is largely represented by wealth, money. Although Congress has the power to create money, to mint it, the greater part of the wealth and the power to create money is actually controlled by a very few individuals. And money is speech.[364]

At this point we should consider the actual possible use of governmental power. At the close of the eighteenth century the monarchs were faced with two heterogeneous groups of persons who could lend support, now loosely nominated as the Aristocrats and the Democrats, or in socialist terms, Aristocrats and Bourgeoisie.

We are not fond of the latter term, bourgeoisie, because that denotes a distinction that was then very possibly unwarranted in certain portions of the western world and merely clothes the future development of power under three theoretical economic categories,

---

[364] Buckley v. Valeo, (1976) 424 U.S. 1, 96 S. Ct. 612; 46 L. Ed. 2d 659; 1976 U.S. LEXIS 16; 76-1 U.S. Tax Cas. (CCH) P9189; Citizens United v. Federal Election Commission, (2010) 558 U.S. 310, 130 S.Ct. 876, 175 L. Ed. 2d 753; McCutcheon v. Federal Election Commission, (2014) 572 U.S. ___,134 S.Ct. 1434

Capitalism, Socialism and Communism. These, for our purposes, confuse the purpose or use of social power: to wit, the aristocracy, the bourgeoisie and the proletariat (formerly the peasant - but now literate and industrialized - to meet the requirements of the industrial world). It confines us to certain economic religions that may blind us to consideration of the ultimate use, benefits and injuries of social power.

We must in all interdisciplinary legal analysis, difficult as it may be, try to come back to analysis of substantial relations of real people, their inherent values, and needs of health, food, shelter, freedom from fear, and the blessings of life, liberty and prosperity, not merely some language equations that generally benefit a few.

What the monarchy was faced with was: (1) it had become or was becoming through history, the common symbol of the sovereignty of a geographical group of people, hopefully, though not always, with some commonalities of language and religion; (2) the powers to be exercised for this geographical group of people were common powers; (3) common power had to be exercised by someone or some entity; (4) the only common receptacle of the national power commonly accepted was the sovereign, who was the symbol and seat of the nation or the commonwealth; (5) the man in the hot seat had to decide his modus operandi including how the power was to be exercised and who would exercise it; and (6) If he made the wrong decision he might well lose his power, nation or his head. Furthermore, on his death or abdication, the entire fabric of society could be changed possibly breaking up many dependable, convenient continuities in the lives and plans of the subjects.

Monarchy, because of the concentration of power, has a basic. logistic problem. One person can only do so much in one day. Thus, if there is a smaller group of homogeneous wealthy and powerful men who hopefully were fairly well distributed throughout the territory and nicely formed chains of command, and were allied with the monarch, a single monarch had some chance of stability. Within the realm the monarch, the symbol of the state, depended upon these persons, an oligarchy, to govern. If he vacillates and appears to ignore the existing chain of command, he is faced with two problems: The resentment of the existing potential chain members and the rising expectations of any new order; the exact problem leading to a reign of terror in France.

Fortunately for the colonies, a local and fairly autonomous chain of command, oligarchy, had been established long before the revolution through wealth and power under theories along the lines of King in Parliament. The growing American pre-revolutionary theory was King and Colonial Legislature. The supremacy to carry forward the revolution was easily found in the lower houses of the legislatures. The war was de jure with the King and de facto with Parliament or King in Parliament. More to the point, it was who should rule in and own America and how.

England itself managed to evade a second beheading because of the gradual development of the secondary chain of command through Commons which became, over a very long period of time, the popular based legislature. That was gradually allowed to become a dominant chain of command of sovereignty and originator of its policy. England lost the colonies because it failed to adequately provide and develop this secondary chain of command through state legislatures, but relied upon limited groups, mostly in Parliament, who were not on the scene.

France faced similar failure in the 19th Century. After Napoleon, the legislatures became supreme and probably for the most part remained so until around 1840. The courts, formerly crown instruments, were generally extremely weak until well after 1800. The executive only gradually gained strength. (These are generalizations, obviously, but ones that are fairly well documented though notable exceptions existed.)

England avoided further violent revolution by gradually giving way to the supremacy of the popular branch by expanding the franchise and through various means of increasing the size and scope of inter-social communications, the necessary precursors of an ordered stable state. But its problems in Ireland, like ours in the Civil War, illustrated the basic national problem of agreement on common unity of sovereignty through the popular branch, geographically divided. Geographic diversity can and does tend to accentuate division and separatism.

As a consequence possibly of the sectional factionalism, but certainly resulting from growing unified wealth, we developed a reestablishment of some unified nationalism in the persons of the courts and executives and economically, the armed forces. It would be foolish to deny that all these services are somewhat aristocratic - monarchic institutions, if we must give them social labels. Military officers are still known as Gentlemen, the lowest rank of the nobility. But they are public officers and in the executive, derived from popular chosen offices and not private offices.

The government set up in the federal convention was the model for this development. It was strenuously resisted and, as Jensen has pointed out, only narrowly accepted at the time. There is a good amount of controversy now, as there was at the time, concerning the success of the Articles of Confederation and more recent economic studies do not necessarily support the theory of the states' bankruptcies under that form of government.

Probably the basic problem with the Articles were their failure to establish a visible national unity in some fashion originating from a nationally conscious people. The national government's own credit, and thus nationalization of wealth, was damaged thereby (though some of the states may have been doing nicely).

The Europeans with their Euro have shown some interesting comparisons in the early 21st Century, although they lack the commonality of language that graced the American states. Between 1776 and 1787, the United States had really developed a feeling of national unity not formally displayed by the various governments adopting the Articles through 1781 and for sometime thereafter.

For some reason, most social persons develop the desire to have, as part of the definition of their own existence, a geographical -- social designation to their own existence requiring a certain amount of visible, tangible, present unity for satisfaction.. A State of New York dollar does not satisfy a United States psychologically desired personality. One can call this a basis of the social contract theory, if one likes (which, if one likes B. F. Skinner, one might avoid). The Social Contract Theory was very old at the time of the revolution, and has been used as a basic theory for practically every form of governmental structure.

What is important in this analysis is formulating some workable guidelines resulting in fluent operation of this "social compact." Two underlying thoughts on social restrictions strike us from our historical experience. Visible, kinetic social power will not long be tolerated as exercised, especially visibly, by an unduly concentrated portion of society for their own ends, a group of dominant oligarchs. Nor will it smoothly function if extremely divided in purposes between the many, at least upon the geographic and populous scale of the United States.. The physical problem of communications will break down either approach. At any particular moment there may be dominant and subservient, or perhaps better expressed as operant and respondent members and groups within society. When we use such terms as "titles of nobility", "due process of law", and "equal protection of the laws", we are working within the framework of possible restrictions on the operants and respondents that will hopefully achieve a working balance within human relationships that will limit the inherent dangers of both concentrated and particulate tendencies in human behavior on a social level.

All this we require to be exercised within a framework maximizing individual freedom and responsibility to achieve the survival and achievement of the overall society, coupled with incumbent survival of its species members. It is a constantly challenging juggling act. Hence the need for, at least in appearance, of frequent opportunities to change the players, and a need to instill on all participants some common social values

With this idea in mind, it then becomes interesting to note what the French, as a much more integrated, populous and financially advanced nation at the time, thought of when, in their Constitution of 1791, did to proscribed the powers of privilege:

3 September, 1791

[Preamble]

The National Assembly, wishing to establish the French Constitution upon the principles it has just recognized and declared, abolishes irrevocably the institutions which were injurious to liberty and equality of rights.

Neither nobility, nor peerage, nor hereditary distinctions, nor distinctions of orders, nor feudal regime, nor patrimonial courts, nor any titles, denominations, or prerogatives derived therefrom, nor any order of knighthood, nor any corporations or decorations requiring proofs of nobility or implying distinctions of birth, nor any superiority other than that of public functionaries in the performance of their duties any longer exists.

Neither venality nor inheritance of any public office any longer exists.

Neither privilege nor exception to the law common to all Frenchmen any longer exists for any part of the nation or for any individual.

Neither jurandes nor corporations of professions, arts, and crafts any longer exist.

The law no longer recognizes religious vows or any other obligation contrary to natural rights or the Constitution.[365]

We find in this, the Articles of Confederation, various revolutionary state constitutions, the Agreement of the Free People of England and carried into the Federal Constitution a basic theme which may well be expressed as: Government is not meant to exist to have its functions either exercised by or for the benefits of a few, an oligarchy no matter how formed, at the expense of the many.

---

[365] http://www.historywiz.com/primarysources/const1791text.html

Today we must seriously challenge any single family or any individuals or similar small group that chooses to contribute huge sums, as one family is reported to have threatened of eight hundred million dollars to influence the outcome of the next national elections. The mere existence of such power and wealth challenges the very foundations of our form of government.

We might look upon such concentrations of power in the hands of individuals, the few or some corporations as a public nuisance that should be enjoined. Unless they can prove their public purpose, they aggregations of power, beyond their needs for sustenance could escheat to the state, as Franklin said, Property superfluous to the Conservation of the Individual and the Propagation of the Species, and thus is the. Property of the Public.'[366]

All of the people must be considered as the primary wealth of the community, the society. Their health, education, opportunities all play a roll in defining the value of that wealth both internally and externally. Their health, happiness and welfare are the obligation of the system. Whenever it is not so exercised, the reasonableness of such internal deviations within the society may be challenged, hopefully in the courts -- federal or state, so long as they are responsive to the rights of all the people. Otherwise it may

---

[366] Smyth, Albert Henry, Editor: **The Writings of Benjamin Franklin**. 10 vols. New York: Macmillan Co., 1905--7. Vol 1. Ch 16, Document 12 *Benjamin Franklin letter December 25, 1783 to Robert Morris* http://press-pubs.uchicago.edu/founders/documents/v1ch16s12.html

be challenged in the streets. Private acts of the government, whether exercised by the legislature, executive or the courts, may be challenged where they establish or seek to perpetuate the private power or privilege in a few at the expense of society as a whole.

Among those items suspect are those actions that might seek to continue, concentrate or expand the powers of persons indefinitely or beyond the life of the actual human exercising them unless done in such fashion as may be reasonably necessary to complete his or its close, socially acceptable obligations or relationships, and preserve its community value as far as possible while integrating it into the society, and conforming to the will of the people as may be expressed at the time.

Some specific areas of inquiry might lay in questioning the constitutionality of loans such as the one recently made to Lockheed. Many of the private acts of Congress might be questioned. The IRS might challenge certain exemptions. Narrowness of issuing certificates of convenience and necessity in the carrier fields might be questioned. Certain types of estate planning devices might be without any aid of the courts because such action would tend to confirm unwarranted power concentration (as the courts now refuse to confirm racial covenant restrictions on land planning). Granting special privileges in the use of the internet by not recognizing it as a public utility available equally to all may fall afoul of the nobility restrictions. Perpetual corporations could well be the subject of much inquiry, perhaps periodic review or as it was historically called, visitation, and under some circumstances, if found wanting, with visitations and dissolution resulting in redistribution of their wealth.

In fact the United States has made, and is considering trade pacts that call for private, non-transparent, and very expensive arbitration that could even bind the state and the federal governments and make them responsible for the commercial losses caused by their laws. These will affect their powers to make or to have previously made laws and regulations to protect labor, health, safety of the people and the environment. Such treaties subject both the United States and the States to such expensive private arbitration from which there is no appeal. This exceeds the power of Congress which can only create tribunals inferior to the Supreme Court, Article 1 §8.[367] These private courts do not appear to be inferior to the Supreme Court. They probably violate the Nobility Clauses

Private courts are clearly a historical privilege of Nobility and such treaty clauses can well be challenged as unconstitutional and beyond the power of Congress, the President or the courts to grant because the nobility restrictions are binding on all of the United States and not, like some of our bill of rights, restricted to one or another function..

---

[367] U. S. Constitution Art. 1 §8   The Congress shall have Power...to constitute Tribunals inferior to the supreme Court;...'

Corporations have been given vast powers to effect the life health and welfare of our citizens. We have lost the historical sense of the reason for the State to incorporate persons. Judge Roan of Virginia in the 1809 case of <u>Curries Administrator v. Mutual Assurance Society</u>.[368] set it forth nicely when he said:

> With respect to acts of incorporation, they ought never to be passed, but in consideration of services to be rendered to the public. This is the principle on which such charters are granted even in England; (1 131. Corn. 467) and it holds a fortiori in this country, as our Bill of Rights interdicts all 'exclusive and separate emoluments or privileges from the community, but in consideration of public services'. (Art. 4) It may often be convenient for a set of associated individuals, to have privileges of a corporation bestowed upon them; but if their object is merely private or selfish; if it is detrimental to, or not promotive of the public good, they have no adequate claim upon the legislature for the privilege. "

Accumulation of power has always continued to be suspect. In 1833. R. B. Tarrey, while Secretary of the United States Treasury, in his report to the House of Representatives on his reasons for withdrawal of federal funds from the Bank of the United States, said:[369]

---

[368]Z 4 Hen & M. 315, 11-14 Va. R. 900

[369] 13 Has. Rep. 90:

"It is a fixed principle of our political institutions to guard against unnecessary accumulation of power over persons and property in any hands. But no hands are less worthy to be trusted with it than those of a moneyed corporation. "

A similar conclusion had been reached in 1820 by a special committee appointed to report on the subject of the then distressed and embarrassed economic condition of the state:

"That cause is to be found chiefly in the abuses of the banking system, which abuses consist first in the excessive number of banks, and secondly in their universal bad administration. For the first of these abuses the people have to reproach themselves, for having urged the legislature to depart from that truly republican doctrine, which influenced the deliberations of our early assemblies, and which taught "That the incorporation of monied interests already sufficiently powerful of itself, was but the creation of odious aristocracies, hostile to the spirit of free government, and subversive of the rights and liberties of the people."[370]

Later adoption of anti-trust and restraint of trade laws support these positions. Perhaps they need to be introduced and enforced again to encourage less disparity and personal campaign influence enjoyed by the very wealthy, whether corporate or individual, as compared to that of the average voter.

---

[370] 4 Haz. Rep. 137.

EPILOGUE

SOCIAL RECAPTURE

An aristocracy cannot exist and an oligarchy can exercise no power, unless given the tools to be recognized by its society. It is based upon that recognition of existing conditions that "nobility" is created. The name is unimportant but the existing conditions are the matters that must be of concern. Nobles, aristocrats, oligarchs, plutocrats need a social framework in which to exercise their powers and enjoy their wealth. Without that, it does not exist. There is no extrinsic value in individuals or objects. Wealth abides in the collective intrinsic value of the sentient being members (on earth mostly humans) who recognize it. Wealth derives from the power to recognize it. Thus wealth and its power rely upon and derive from the worth ultimately placed upon the intrinsic value of the collective membership of that society by that society for those who are allowed to exercise it.

Each society then has the obligation, the right and duty, to say how and when it may be enjoyed and used.. While "God" might anoint the King of the Jews,[371] the people had to chose to have one,.

The nobility and related clauses, state and federal, the confiscations during the revolution of properties such as the Pen's unimproved lands, all teach us that part of the foundations of our

---

[371] Deuteronomy 17:14-20 New International Version

238

country, indeed western Democracy with a big D are restrictions on wide disparities of private wealth and power that are or should be discouraged or controlled for the health of society as a whole.

What was done with the confiscated property? It Escheated. It was turned back into the public wheal, the public common treasury for supporting future growth of the people. The principle of public recapture of wealth was established very early in our constitutional history, However, we were a country endowed with such fabulous riches that we allowed this principle to fade into history, largely out of any economic thought and from memory. It is time to revive the basic premise of social recapture and reasonable protection as a foundation and support of our society and reduce any tendency to promote some future noble oligarchy.

John Locke in a work of political philosophy published anonymously in 1689, observed that all that anyone might expect by right by way of inheritance on the death of a parent would be:

> "The right of a Son has to be maintained and provided with the necessities and conveniences of Life out of his Father's Stock, gives him a Right to succeed to his Father's <u>Property</u> for his own good, but this can give him no right to succeed also to the <u>Rule</u>, which his Father had over other Men. All that a Child has a right to claim from his Father is Nourishment and Education, and the things nature furnishes for the support of Life: But he has no Right to demand <u>Rule</u> or <u>Dominion</u>: He can subsist and receive from him the

Portion of good things, and advantages of Education naturally due to him, without <u>Empire</u> and <u>Dominion</u> ....”[372]

We might consider a liberal inheritance to furnish nourishment, health and education as a possible right. But beyond that, larger inheritances, distinguishing heirs rights as superior to those of the community are in question because those rights can only exist if granted by the community. The dead owner has lost control and he or she has relinquished that control to the community. The community may only grant that control to heirs in a limited fashion, without creating unacceptable disparities whether recognized through probate, contract, corporate or trust provisions, or intestate descent. All require State recognition to be enforced. Any further grants by the community should be clearly for community purposes and continual responsibility to that community. Beyond that we create an oligarchy, aristocracy, plutocracy, a nobility

If a person died with X value in the property owned or controlled at his or her death, how much could the state allow him or her to direct to others without considering it a grant of Titles of Nobility. If he is 100 times richer than the average, is any grant within that 100 times richer permissible? Would, for example, the grant of inheritance of a sustainable family farm (not a factory farm), one that could provide sustenance to a family to encourage

---

[372] John Locke: **Two Treatises of Government**, I §97, Peter Laslett, Ed. Cambridge University Press (1963) p. 250.

its continued use, be within bounds of social acceptance? Possibly so, provided it were to be worked as a family farm. Would that allow valued inheritance up to three to five million dollars in today's market economy? Possibly so. But these are matters for serious public discussion and democratic decisions.

Also to be decided is what may be the best way for any recapture to be recovered. One does not want to destroy the wealth recovered. One wants to try to recover it at its full market value so that its full values may be shared through the community, and lives may not be seen as lived in vain. Certainly the producers of such wealth, in providing for their own legacy, should be entitled to have some say in this, perhaps as the charitable work of Carnegie in the nineteenth century, or today the Gates family illustrates. These producers can begin this wholesome recapture in their life times. Those who retain what they have taken out of the economy in wide disparity to the rest of the population can contribute to this recapture through taxation.

And where should it go? Again these are matters for public debate. But we should consider establishing a base level of economic stability for each member of the community and participant in the society, to provide the freedoms, as Franklin D. Roosevelt said during World War II: Freedom from want and fear: provision for shelter, food on the table, health care, and opportunities to learn and thrive.

Indeed, Jefferson, Franklin and Locke gave us the western and American basis of an jury instruction and judicial question to be determined before such property escheats, and should be reclaimed by Society. Such a reclamation would not be a taking under the fifth or fourteenth amendment but merely a re-exertion of society's control over what already belongs to it. A typical instruction or legal premise might read:

> Is the Property superfluous to the conservation of the individual and the Propagation of the Species (Franklin) and where it has not been earned by the clamant, and is not for the nourishment, health and education, or an individual (Locke) and in the case of the partnership, corporation or business trust, not the direct investment of the partners, shareholders, or beneficiaries and its earnings that may not be attributed to such investments but to other advantages; then this generation of this government is not bound to recognize it as the property of the claimant and it may escheat it to the state and the community (Jefferson) to which it rightly belongs.[373]

[373] Franklin: Smyth, Albert Henry, Editor: **The Writings of Benjamin Franklin**. 10 vols. New York: Macmillan Co., 1905--7. Vol 1. Ch 16, Document 12 *Benjamin Franklin letter December 25, 1783 to Robert Morris* http://press-pubs.uchicago.edu/founders/documents/v1ch16s12.html ; Locke: John Locke: **Two Treatises of Government**, I §97, Peter Laslett, Ed. Cambridge University Press (1963) p. 250; and Jefferson: *Thomas Jefferson to Thomas Earle. September 24, 1823* http://www.yamaguchy.com/library/jefferson/1823.html **The Writings of Thomas Jefferson,** editor H.A. Washington New York : H.W. Derby, 1861; and *Thomas Jefferson to John Wayles Eppes, 1813*. Saul K.

The most painless and logical moment to exercise recapture is the moment of death when property has lost its real ownership. The ownerships provided after death of the individual are all artificial and exist by sufferance or promotion of the state, hence can be seen as the State's "grant" that can be, according to power, privileges allowed, the seeds of great disparity in living conditions, and special protections provided in that "grant." These can be considered as prohibited granting of Titles of Nobility. It will also be wise to restrict the nature of gifts beyond such purposes.

We can also exercise the power when a member of this plutocracy, oligarchy, nobility decides that he, she or it will so exercise his, hers or its powers to influence or control the political and social orders of the society in a fashion for beyond the means of the ordinary adult individuals in that society, legally or illegally, or use it to perform some illegal act. This exercise of power could be attacked under such legal theories as public nuisances unless or until our legislatures wish to define the task more precisely. But the right should continue to be maintained in the hands of the people.

Padover, ed. **Thomas Jefferson on Democracy** (13th Printing) pp 15, 16. See also Memorial Edition, Ford Edition 13:169, http://famguardian.org/Subjects/Politics/ThomasJefferson/jeff1340.htm; and *Thomas Jefferson To: John W. Eppes, June 24, 1813*, http://illinoisconservative.com/Jefferson/tj-public-debt-1.html

This would give us a new vision of society, not one torn by disparities if wealth, inheritance and opportunity limits dependant on birth, but rather where one may feel more confident that all are truly valued by, can participate in and may thrive in our common Democratic society. These ideas can hardly be considered "un-American" as they are part of the founding of the United States and illustrate its goals in valuing its people. They are written into our basic law to be exercised by the people and their representatives for the benefit of all.

Finally there is the matter of the corporation. Massachusetts Trust and other more permanent institutions that have no natural death to act as triggers to revolve their powers or wealth.

The corporation is a creature of the state. As such its primary purpose is and always has been to act for the public good. That has been its primary duty historically and continues to be so today. The profit corporation does not exist today to maximize shareholder values and profits.[374]

In many ways it resembles the Palatine nobility and grand Dukes of the past, but without the traditional social responsibilities of providing protection, local governance and sustenance. But without the requirement of being primarily for the public good, it is little more that raw, oligarchical power with limited responsibility

---

[374] See for example Lynn A. Stout, Cornell Law School, recent work **The Shareholder Value Myth: How Putting Shareholders First Harms Investors, Corporations, and the Public** (2012)

for its actions. Such a grant of power could certainly appear to cross the prohibitions of granting titles of nobility by using this enormous state power for aggregating and directing wealth for purely private purposes and even beyond that without the accompanying liability to the owners. Shareholders, for its failure or misuse of its powers.

The state continues to insure this action throughout the corporate existence and is vested with life and death powers of enforcement and correction by using dissolution and lesser actions such as specific restrictions, fines, visitation and direction.

Were a corporation to offend like British Petroleum did in the Gulf of Mexico and either plead or be found guilty of criminal violations, it would be entirely reasonable for the state, through the courts, to appoint visitors for as long as necessary with full powers of all the board members to go into the corporation, at its own expense, to determine the problems, discover any wrong doers, expose any further criminal actions and generally investigate to hold the corporation, its directors, officers, employees and representatives accountable for its public duties and make public reports back to the court and the state.

Corporations are great accumulators and repositories of wealth. while safeguarding owners from social and legal responsibilities. Society may consider this useful so long as the corporations are providing a public service. But they may be limited in the distributions of this wealth in order to avoid very wide disparities in income from the production of the corporations. Realistic levels of wealth distribution to encourage useful leadership, efforts and accomplishments could be encouraged while exceeding these level could be discouraged through Taxation or other programs, perhaps those suggested here.

Indeed the States and the United States should consider establishing offices of corporate visitation to be available to the courts and other regulatory agencies for use when all corporations, both foreign and domestic, plead or are found guilty of violating the law. Outside of some small tax to maintain the state office of visitation, the corporations should have no complaint over the costs or inconvenience of such visitation as long as such corporations do not violate the law.

The public duty to make money and return profits to the shareholders is but one of the "for profit" corporate responsibilities and this is always secondary to the corporation's duty to obey the law and exercise its charter for the public good. This should be required to be taught in every state business education institution and law school and enforced in every court and regulatory agency. State appointed visitors should be under the most stringent fiduciary duty to avoid any conflicts of interest and face severe penalties if they fail to exercise reasonable care to report any further or future corporate misdeeds or violate their fiduciary duty to the State in any way.

We must remember we do not change social, political and economic reality by merely changing the language, the name tags. Nobility, Oligarchy, Plutocracy and Aristocracy or what ever term is used, identifies unrestrained powers of a few that can be and often are detrimental to the interests of humanity as a whole and the danger is in the existence of such power.

Bibliography

Adams, John   and Jonathan Sewell **Novanglus and Massachusettensis** Reproduction of 1819 edition (Russell & Rusell, 1968)

Adrian Tinniswood,

http://www.nytimes.com/2010/07/04/opinion/04tinniswood.html?_r=0

Agreement of the People (1648) from **John Lilburn Foundations of Freedom**

American Law Journal (1809)

Anderson James Donald; *Vandalia: The First West Virginia?* West Virginia History Vol. 40, No. 4 (Summer 1979), pp. 375-92

http://en.wikipedia.org/wiki/Vandalia_(colony)

Andrews, James Dewitt: **American Law. A Commentary on the Jurisprudence, Constitution and Laws of the United States** (2 ed 1908) Vol I

Antifederalist Paper No. 9 – **A Consolidated Government Is a Tyranny**,
http://www.thefederalistpapers.org/antifederalist-paper-9

Antifederalist Paper No. 40 *On the Motivations and Authority of the Founding Fathers*
http://www.rightsofthepeople.com/freedom_documents/anti_federalist_papers/anti_federalist_papers_40.php

Antifederalist Paper No. 1 General Introduction: *A Dangerous Plan of Benefit Only to the Aristocratick Combination* From The Boston Gazette and Country Journal, November 26, 1787

http://www.rightsofthepeople.com/freedom_documents/anti_federalist_papers/anti_federalist_papers_01.php

Ashe, S. A.; **History of North Carolina.**

Ashton, T.S.; **An Economic History of England: The Eighteenth Century**, (Methven & Co. Ltd., London, reprint 1955)

Balkin, J.M.; *The Constitution of Status*, 106 YALE L.J. 2313, 2350 (1996) citing Gordon S.
Wood, **The Radicalism of the American Revolution** (1992) pp. 41-42

Bancroft, George; **History of the Formation of the Constitution**, vol. ii,

Barnes, Viola Florence. **The Dominion of New England: A Study in British Colonial Policy** (1923)

Bassett, John Spencer ; **A Short History of the United States** (2d ed 1924), p. 76

Blackstone, William; **Commentaries on the Laws of England**...(hereinafter BC) A Facsimile of the First Edition of 1765-69 (Oxford, Clarendon Press), University of Chicago Press,' 1979 Vol. 1

Bond, Jr., Beverley W.; **Introduction to the Quit-rent System in the American Colonies**. Yale University Press (1919)

Bond, Jr.. Beverley W.; **Quit-rent System in the American Colonies** Yale University Press (1919)

Boyd, Paul J et al, editors **The Papers of Thomas Jefferson**. Princeton: Princeton University Press, 1950

Breen, T. H.; **The Character of a Good Ruler, Puritan Political Ideas in New England 1630-1730** W.W. Norton, © Yale University 1970

Brewer, Willkis: **Brewer's Alabama History** 1540-1872.Montgomery, AL, USA: Barrett & Brown, 1872.

Bridenbaugh , Carl; **Cities in Revolt** (Oxford University Press 1971)

Bridenbaugh,, Carl; **Mitre and Septer** (Oxford University Press, 1967)

Brown, John; **Estimate of the Manner and Principles of the Times**, 2 Vols. 1757,

Brown, Richard D.; **Revolutionary Politics in Massachusetts** (Harvard U. Pr. 1970, Norton Library 1976)

Burke, Edmund; *Letter to Duke of Richmond* (November 17, 1772)
http://www.fullbooks.com/Burke1.html **Letters of Edmund Burke** selection No. 155. Henry Library /World Classics, CCXXVII Edited, with introduction by Harold J. Laski

Bush, Michael; **European Nobility, Vol. I. Noble Privilege**, Holmes A Neier Publishers, Inc., London 1982

Butterfield, L.H., editor, Leonard C. Faber and Wendell D. Garrett, Assistant editors; **The Adams Papers, Diary & Autobiography of John Adams, Vol. I,** (Atheneum, originally published by Harvard U. Pr., New York 1964)

Butterfield L.H., editor in chief, L. Kinvin Wroth and Hiller B. Zobel, editors, **The Adams Papers, .Legal Papers of John Adams**, Atheneum, 1968, originally published by Harvard U. Press, 1964) Vol, Vol II

Cadwalader, Richard McCall, **A Practical Treatise on Law of Ground Rents in Pennsylvania**,

http://www.ancestry.com/wiki/index.php?title=Delaware_Land_Records

Campbell, Edward D.: **Filibuster Solution: The People's Answer to The Senate's Super Majority Rules or Returning the Senate to The States and the People** (2011)

Canavan, Francis; **The Political Economy of Edmund Burke, The Role of Property in His Thought**, Fordham University Press, 1995

Centinel http://www.constitution.org/afp/centin00.htm

Christian, Edward, Editor; **Blackstone's Commentaries of the Law of England** (1765), Philadelphia 1825 Book I,

Colburn, H. Trevor; **The Lamp of Experience. Whig history and the Intellectual Origins of the American Revolution**; The Norton Library, 1974

Coleman, Nannie McCormick; **The Constitution and its Framers**, Chicago, 1910,

Cooley: Thomas M.: **Constitutional Limitations** (6th ed. 1890)

Corwin, Edward S.: **The Constitution of the United States of America, Analysis and Interpretation** (1952)

Crosskey,William Winslow :**Politics and the Constitution** (1955 ed)

Curry: Cecil B.; **Road to Revolution, Benjamin Franklin in England 1765-1775** (Doubleday Anchor Original 1968)

Delgado, Richard; *Inequality "From the Top": Applying an Ancient Prohibition to an Emerging Problem of Distributive Justice*, 32 UCLA L. Rev. 100, 114 (1984).

Documents Illustrative of The Foundation of the Union of American States (69th Congress, 1st Session House Document No. 378)

Deuteronomy 17:14-20 New International Version

Edwards, John; **Christian Córdoba: The city and its region in the late Middle Ages**, Cambridge University Press (1982)

Elliot, Jonathan; Madison, James: Commentaries on The Constitution of The United States of America ..., 1866

http://books.google.com/books?id=OS4MAQAAMAAJ&pg=PA150&lpg=PA150&dq=Another+great+advantage,+sir,+in+the+constitution+before+us,+is,+its+excluding+all+titles+of+nobility+or+hereditary+succession+of+power;+which+hath+been+a+main+engine+of+tyranny+in+foreign+countries.&source=bl&ots=FwRWYXCxz5&sig=dX7QIREvflmZ1Hs3IHMSq8DgUMY&hl=en&sa=X&ei=yhfkU6OiHor5oATnvIHwDA&ved=0CBQQ6AEwAA#v=onepage&q=Another%20great%20advantage%2C%20sir%2C%20in%20the%20constitution%20before%20us%2C%20is%2C%20its%20excluding%20all%20titles%20of%20nobility%20or%20hereditary%20succession%20of%20power%3B%20which%20hath%20been%20a%20main%20engine%20of%20tyranny%20in%20foreign%20countries.&f=false

Elliot, Jonathan **The Debates in the Several State Conventions on the Adoption of the Federal Constitution** 2d Ed Vol III, *The Debates in the Convention of the Commonwealth of Virginia, On the Adoption of the Federal Constitution. June 11, 1788,*

http://www.constitution.org/rc/rat_va_09.htm

Elliot, Jonathan, Editor, **The Debates in the Several State Conventions on the Adoption of etc...**, Volume 2

Harper, Douglass . **Emancipation in Massachusetts**

. http://slavenorth.com/massemancip.htm

http://books.google.com/books?id=EjEMAQAAMAAJ&pg=PA269&lpg=PA2
69&dq=But,+says+the+gentlemen,+the+rich+will+be+always+brought+forwa
rd:+they+will+exclusively+enjoy+the+suffrages+of+the+people.&source=bl&
ots=JEXhDp30xq&sig=GdHfD9zGW3Cec1zz5RABz3wIPL4&hl=en&sa=X&
ei=-SDkU_DJC86BogSM6IHoCg&ved=0CBQQ6AEwAA#v=onepage&q=Bu
t%2C%20says%20the%20gentlemen%2C%20the%20rich%20will%20be%20a
lways%20brought%20forward%3A%20they%20will%20exclusively%20enjoy
%20the%20suffrages%20of%20the%20people.&f=false

Farrand, Max, Editor; **The Records of the Federal Convention of 1787**, Yale
U. Press, 1911, Vol I,

Ferguson, John H., and Dean L. Henry, **The American System of
Government** (1953)

Fourquin, Guy; **Lordship and Feudalism in the Middle Ages**, translated by
Iris and A. L. Lytton Sells, Pica Pres 1976 © George Allen & Ubwin Ltd.

Freeland, Chrystia; **Plutocrats: The Rise of the New Global Super-Rich and
the Fall of Everyone Else**, Paperback – 2013

Gardner, Samuel Rawson; **The Constitutional Documents of the Puritan
Revolution** 1625-1660 (3rd revised ed. Oxford University press reprint 1968)

Goodwin, Albert, Editor; **The European Nobility in the Eighteenth Century**
(Harper Torchbooks, 1967)

Gosling, G.R. Printer; **The Laws of Honour or a Compendious Account of
the Ancient Derivation of all Titles, Dignities, Offices, Etc, as Well as
Temporal, Civil or Military**. (sold by John Osborn, 1726)

Gosling,, G.R., printer; **The Laws of Honour or a Compendious Account of the Ancient Derivation of all Titles, Dignities, Offices, Etc, as Well as Temporal Civil or Military.** (sold by John Osborn 1726)

Graves, M.A.R.; *Freedom of. Peers from Arrest*, 21 AM.j.L.Hist. 1 (1977)

Habakkuk, H. John; **Marriage, debt, and the estates system: English landownership 1650–1950** (Oxford: Clarendon Press, 1994).

Habakkuk, H. J.; **England**

Haller, William and Godfrey Davis, Editors **The Leveller Tracts 1647-1653** (1944)

Halsbury's Laws of England (Third Ed.)

Harper. Douglass; **Emancipation in Massachusetts**.

http://slavenorth.com/massemancip.htm

http://www.michaelariens.com/ConLaw/justices/cushing.htm

Hay, Douglas; *Poaching and the Game Laws on Caneock Chase* in

Albion's Fatal. Tree. Crime and Society in the Eighteenth Century England

(Pantheon Books, 1975);

Headrick, William Cecil; *A Study of Social Stratification With Reference to Social Class Barriers and Social Class Rigidity* Doctoral dissertation, Doctor of Philosophy at New York State University. December 1, 1941.

http://en.wikipedia.org/wiki/History_of_slavery_in_Massachusetts

http://alfredjordanpacheco.com/ajp19.htm

http://avalon.law.yale.edu/17th_century/mass01.asp

http://avalon.law.yale.edu/17th_century/mass02.asp;

http://avalon.law.yale.edu/17th_century/mass03.asp;

http://avalon.law.yale.edu/17th_century/mass07.asp

http://avalon.law.yale.edu/17th_century/me01.asp

http://avalon.law.yale.edu/17th_century/nc01.asp

http://avalon.law.yale.edu/17th_century/nc04.asp

http://avalon.law.yale.edu/17th_century/nh04.asp

http://avalon.law.yale.edu/17th_century/nh05.asp;

http://avalon.law.yale.edu/17th_century/nj04.asp

http://avalon.law.yale.edu/17th_century/ri04.asp

http://avalon.law.yale.edu/17th_century/va03.asp

http://avalon.law.yale.edu/18th_century/ga01.asp

ttp://avalon.law.yale.edu/18th_century/nc07.asp

http://avalon.law.yale.edu/18th_century/nj14.asp

http://avalon.law.yale.edu/18th_century/pa08.asp

http://avalon.law.yale.edu/18th_century/proc1763.asp

http://avalon.law.yale.edu/18th_century/vt01.asp

http://docsouth.unc.edu/nc/conv1788/conv1788.xml

http://en.cyclopaedia.net/wiki/William-Grant-(seigneur)

http://en.wikipedia.org/wiki/Baron

http://en.wikipedia.org/wiki/Battle_of_Roncevaux_Pass_(778)

http://en.wikipedia.org/wiki/Charles_Lynch_(jurist)

http://en.wikipedia.org/wiki/Claverack,_New_York

http://en.wikisource.org/wiki/Constitution_of_the_Commonwealth_of_Massachusetts_(1780)

http://en.wikipedia.org/wiki/Canadian_peers_and_baronets

http://en.wikipedia.org/wiki/Hellfire_Club

http://en.wikipedia.org/wiki/Henry_V

http://en.wikipedia.org/wiki/Henry_Vane_the_Younger

http://en.wikipedia.org/wiki/James_Oglethorpe

http://en.wikipedia.org/wiki/Canadian_peers_and_baronets

http://en.wikipedia.org/wiki/John_Carteret,_2nd_Earl_Granville

http://en.wikipedia.org/wiki/John_Lilburne

http://en.wikipedia.org/wiki/Livingston_Manor
http://en.wikipedia.org/wiki/History_of_slavery_in_Massachusetts

http://en.wikipedia.org/wiki/Manorialism

http://en.wikipedia.org/wiki/Ohio_Company

http://en.wikipedia.org/wiki/Palatine

http://en.wikipedia.org/wiki/Patroon

http://en.wikipedia.org/wiki/Quebec_Act

http://en.wikipedia.org/wiki/Quit-rent

https://en.wikipedia.org/wiki/Roman_aristocracy

http://en.wikipedia.org/wiki/Royal_Proclamation_of_1763

http://en.wikipedia.org/wiki/Seigneurial_system_of_New_France;

http://en.wikipedia.org/wiki/State_cessions

http://en.wikipedia.org/wiki/Temple_Baronets

http://en.wikipedia.org/wiki/Thomas_Temple

http://en.wikipedia.org/wiki/Treaty_of_Fort_Stanwix

http://en.wikipedia.org/wiki/Treaty_of_Lochaber

http://en.wikipedia.org/wiki/Vandalia_(colony)

http://en.wikipedia.org/wiki/William_Grant_(seigneur).

http://famguardian.org/Subjects/Politics/ThomasJefferson/jeff1340.htm

http://founders.archives.gov/documents/Franklin/01-23-02-0094

http://globalgenealogy.com/globalgazette/gazbm/gazbm057.htm

http://illinoisconservative.com/Jefferson/tj-public-debt-1.html

http://libro.uca.edu/vassberg/land4.htm

http://papers.ssrn.com/sol3/papers.cfm?abstract_id=680661

http://patmos.tripod.com/qc/hs408p1.html

http://readtheconstitutionstupid.com/en/?option=com_content&view=article&id=2369:1689-boston-declaration-of-grievances-April-18-1689&catid=130&Itemid=744&lang=en;

http://richardjohnbr.blogspot.com/2010/10/Seignuerial-system-and-settlement.html

http://search.findwide.com/serp?guid={D3B40CB8-7BA8-4CA5-A59B-3BB107B6DA2C}&action=default_search&serpv=22&k=Lieutenant-Colonel+Gabriel+Christie

http://teachingamericanhistory.org/library/document/objections-to-the-constitution/

http://thecanadianencyclopedia.com/en/article/Seignuerial-system/

http://www.anti-slaverysociety.addr.com/hus-mass.htm

http://www.britannica.com/EBchecked/topic/491019/Edward-Randolph

http://www.earlyamerica.com/earlyamerica/milestones/commonsense/text.html

http://www.earlyamerica.com/ebooks/books/FathersOfConstitution/FathersOfConstitution.html

http://www.csawardept.com/documents/Constitutions/CSA/Provisional/index.html

http://www.germanculture.com.ua/library/history/bl_habsburgs.htm

http://www.magnoliabuzz.com/books/brewer/al-county-dallas-saffold2.php

http://www.masshist.org/endofslavery/index.php?id=54

http://www.mongabay.com/reference/country_studies/spain/HISTORY.html

http://www.nhinet.org/ccs/docs/va-1776.htm

http://www.nhinet.org/ccs/docs/ny-1777.htm

http://www.northcarolinahistory.org/commentary/121/entry

http://www.offshore-manual.com/taxhavens/Sark.html

http://www.u-s-history.com/pages/h1160.htm

http://www.virginiaplaces.org/settleland/fairfaxgrant.html#two

http://saffold.com/history/?p=6

http://users.humboldt.edu/ogayle/hist110/colonialdiscontent.html

Hume, David ; **The History of England from the Invasion of Julius Caesar to the Abdication of James the Second**, 1688) Boston 1854 Vol IV

Innes. Stephen; **Labor in New England, Economy and Society in Seventeenth Century Springfield**, Princeton University Press ©1983

Intergenerational Justice in the United States Constitution, The Stewardship Doctrine: III. Constitutional Text, B *Prohibitions of Nobility - modern American society*. Constitutional Law Foundation, 50 West 36th Street, Eugene, Oregon 97405
http://www.conlaw.org/Intergenerational-III-2-4.htm

Jackson Turner Main, **The Social Structure of Revolutionary America** (1965)

Jacobson, David L., Editor; **The English Libertarian Heritage from the Writings of John Trenchard and Thomas Gordon in The Independent Whig and Cato's Letters**. (Bobbs_Merrill Co., The American Heritage Series 1965)

Jarrett, Derek; **England in the Age of Hogarth** (1974) (Paladin 1976)

Jarrett, Derek; **The Begetters of Revolution, England's Involvement with France 1759--1789**, Longman Group Ltd., London 1973

Jefferson, Thomas to Thomas Earle. September 24, 1823
 http://www.yamaguchy.com/library/jefferson/1823.html

Jensen, Merril, Ed.itor **Tracts of The American Revolution 1763-1776** (1967)

Journal of Continental Congress, Vol. V

Karst, Kenneth L.; *The Fifth Amendment Guarantee of Equal Protection*, N.C.L. Rev. 55:541 (April 1977)

Kenyon, J. P.; **The Stuart Constitutional Documents and Commentary** (Cambridge University Press reprint 1973)

Kickler, Troy L.; **North Carolina History Project, Quitrents (Colonial Period)**
http://www.northcarolinahistory.org/commentary/121/entry

Larson, Carlton F.W.: *Titles of Nobility,Hereditary Privilege, and the Unconstitutionality of Legacy Preferences in Public School Admissions*, 4 Wash. U. L. R. 1375, 1381, 1401-02, 1408 (2006)

Lee, Richard Henry: *Letters from the Federal Farmer to the Republican III October 10th, 1787.* http://www.constitution.org/afp/fedfar03.txt

Lee, Jr., Charles Robert; **The Confederate Constitutions** (1963)

Lee, Richard Henry; **Letters From The Federal Farmer** Letter XVI (January 20, 1788) Editor McDonald, Forrest (Indianapolis: Liberty Fund 1999).

Accessed from http://oll.libertyfund.org/title/690/102320

Leigh, Oliver H. G., Editor. **The Federalist Papers**. 1901, Universal Classics Library, Vol.I and II

Life in the Early Middle Colonies, New York, New Jersey, Pennsylvania, Delaware, Vermont. A General Historical Survey

http://www.rootsweb.ancestry.com/~nycoloni/dahistmc.html

Locke, John; *The Fundamental Constitutions of Carolina, (1669)*

http://www.constitution.org/jl/funconcar.html

Locke, John; **Two Treatises of Government, I §97,** Peter Laslett, Editor Cambridge University Press (1963)

Lundberg, Ferdinand; **The Rich and the Super-Rich: A Study in the Power of Money, 1968.**

Madison, James **The Debates in the Several State Conventions on the Adoption of The Constitution,** *Volume 4,*

http://books.google.com/books?id=ccfZAAAAMAAJ&pg=PA323&lpg=PA 323&dq=I+am+led+to+conclude,+that+mediocrity+of+fortune+is+a+lead ing+feature+in+our+national+character&source=bl&ots=Kc_OFR_qLD &sig=gVJz76HnQFaCi3zMunppWfD8fCE&hl=en&sa=X&ei=iRLkU5jjIo _8oATejYKwCA&ved=0CBkQ6AEwAQ#v=onepage&q=I%20am%20led% 20to%20conclude%2C%20that%20mediocrity%20of%20fortune%20is%2

0a%20leading%20feature%20in%20our%20national%20character&f=false

Main,Jackson Turner; The Anti Federalist (W.W. Norton & Co., Inc. N.Y. 1961) (Norton Paperback 1964)

Main, Jackson Turner; **The Social Structure of Revolutionary America**. ... Princeton University Press, 1965

Mannix, Daniel. **The Hell Fire Club. London:** Simon and Schuster, 2001

Maryland Farmer and Planter; **The Antifederalist Papers No. 26** *The Use of Coercion by the New Government* (Part I), Maryland Journal and Baltimore Advertiser, April 1, 1788.

Maxwell, William B. *"Washington's Western Lands."* e-WV: The West Virginia Encyclopedia. 13 November 2013. Web. 01 February 2014.

http://www.wvencyclopedia.org/articles/2344

McCrady, Edward; **The History of South Carolina Under the Proprietary Government;**

McKean, Thomas; Wilson, James **Commentaries on the Constitution of the United States of America:** By Pennsylvania. Convention,

http://books.google.com/books?id=LaxbAAAAQAAJ&pg=PA129&lpg=PA129&dq=What+particular+rights+have+been+reserved+to+any+class+of+men,+or+any+occasion.+Does+even+the+first+magistrate+of+the+United+States+draw+to+himself+a+single+privilege&source=bl&ots=rYrjkM6MsE&sig=x6IXX6v79N6JIwms0cwELbjkL_8&hl=en&sa=X&ei=OxXkU8yGLc67oQTy44KYAQ&ved=0CBQQ6AEwAA#v=onepage&q=What%20particular%20rights%20have%20been%20reserved%20to%20any%20class%20of%20men%2C%20or%20any%20occasion.%20Does%20even%20the%20first%20magistrate%20of%20the%20United%20States%20draw%20to%20himself%20a%20single%20privilege&f=false

Merriwether, R. T.; **Dictionary of American History Vol. I,** James Thurlow Adams, Editor in Chief, Charles Scribner, 1940.

Mingay, G.E.; **English Landed Society in the Eighteenth Century,** Routledge Kegan Paul Ltd., 1963

Montezuma; **The Antifederalist Papers No. 27, The Use of Coercion by the New Government (Part I), "** October 29, 1787 Philadelphia, Independent Gazetteer

Moore, Frank V.; **Diary of The American Revolution** (New York 1865) Vol I

Morton, A. L. , Editor. **Freedom in Arms** (Lawwrence & Wishart, ltd. London 1975

Naylor, John F., Editor; **The British Aristocracy and the Peerage Bill of 1719** (Oxford University Press, 1968)

Nelson, Jeffrey M.; *Ideology in Search of a Context: Eighteenth Century British Political Thought and the Loyalists of the American Revolution,* **The Historical Journal 20, 3 (Sept. 1977)**

No l, Francoise; **Christie Seigneuries: Estate Management and Settlement in the Upper Richelieu Valley, 1760-1854,** McGill-Queen's Press - MQUP, Apr 1, 1992

Old South Leaflets

Olson-Raymer, Dr. **History 110 -** *Colonial Discontent*

http://users.humboldt.edu/ogayle/hist110/colonialdiscontent.html

Padover, Saul K. Editor**. Thomas Jefferson n Democracy (13**[th] **Printing),** *Thomas Jeferson to John Wayles Eppes, 1813.* (©1947)

Page, E. & Pendleton, C. V. & C.. **1 Withe 211, 215,** 1 VRA 221, 222 (1793)

Paine, Thomas**; pamphlet Agrarian Justice, 1797 English translation.**
http://www.ssa.gov/history/tpaine3.html

Painter, Sidney**; Studies In The History of the English Feudal Barony,** The Johns Hopkins University Studies In Historical and Social Science Series LXI Number 3, 1943

Palmer, R.. R.**; The Age of Democratic Revolution,** Princeton University Press (1969) vol. I

Pinot-Duclos, Charles; **Considerations sur les Moers,** suprs. pp. 24-25, Cambridge : University Press, 1939 (French)

Plumb, J. H.**; The First Four Georges** (Little, Brown & Co., Boston, Toronto 1975)

Power. Garrett: **Calvert vs. Carroll The Quit-Rent Controversy Between Maryland's Founding Families. .(2005)**
http://papers.ssrn.com/sol3/papers.cfm?abstract_id=680661

Proc. of Mass. Hist. Soc., Volume 1873-1875 Pages: p. 292-295.

Raithby, John Editor (1819) **[1642].** *Charles I, 1640: An Act for disinabling all persons in Holy Orders to exercise any temporall jurisdiccion or authoritie.* **Statutes of the Realm. 5 (1628-80)**

Rapin, Paul de, **History of England with notes by N. Tindal, Vol. XII** (London 1730)

Rawle, William; **A View of the Constitution of the United States 2**nd **Ed.** 1829,

Robinson:, W. A.; **Dictionary of American History Vol. IV,** James Thurlow Adams, Editor in Chief, Charles Scribner, 1940

Rowland, Kate Mason; **The Life of George Mason 1725-1792** (New York 1892) Vol. I,

Rude, George; **Europe in the Eighteenth Century, Aristocracy and the Bourgeois Challenge (1972) (Praeger 1973)**

Rush, Benjamin; **Observations upon the Present Government of Pennsylvania** 8 (Phila., Styner & Cist 1777).

Rushworth, John; **Collections (1721)**

Rutland, Robert Allen: **The Birth of the Bill of Rights, 1776-1791** (2011) Literary Licensing, LLC

Selden, Joyn; **Titles of Honour 3rd ed,** Printed by E. Tyler and R. Holt, for Thomas Eacsett. 1672

Shade, Gary; **Antifederalist Papers, No. 36** *Representation and Internal Taxation.*

http://www.firearmsandliberty.com/Antifederalist/TheAntiFederalistPapers.pdf

Shelburn Papers, 72:311; William L. Clements Library

Silversmith, Jol A.; *Missing Thirteenth Amendment": Constitutional Nonsense and Titles of Nobility.* 8 Southern California Interdisciplinary Law Journal 577 (April 1999)

Simmons, R.C.; *Class Ideology and Revolutionary War* History 62, 204 pp. 62-70 (Feb. 1977),

Smith, William Henry, editor, **St. Clair Papers, Vol. I** *Thomas Smith to Maj. General Arthur St. Clair* (Robert Clark Co. 1882) Vol. I,

Smyth, Albert Henry, Editor: **The Writings of Benjamin Franklin. 10 vols.** New York: Macmillan Co., 1905--7. **Vol 1. Ch 16, Document 12** *Benjamin Franklin letter December 25, 1783 to Robert Morris*
 http://press-pubs.uchicago.edu/founders/documents/v1ch16s12.html

Somers **Collection of Tracts (2nd Ed. London 1818 Vol. VI)** *The True Portraiture of Kings of England*

Steele, Ian K.; *Origins of Boston's Revolutionary Declaration of 18 April 1689,* The New England Quarterly, Vol. 62, No. 1 (Mar., 1989)

Storing, Herbert J., Editor; **The Founders' Constitution** Volume 1, Chapter 13, Document 37
http://press-pubs.uchicago.edu/founders/documents/v1ch13s37.html

Stout, Lynn A.; **The Shareholder Value Myth: How Putting Shareholders First Harms Investors, Corporations, and the Public** (2012)

The University of Chicago Press. **The Complete Anti-Federalist 7 vols.** Chicago: University of Chicago Press, 1981

Story, Joseph: **Commentaries on the Constitution of the United States,** (5th Ed. 1891)

Sunstein, Cass R.: *The Anticaste Principle,* Mich. L. Rev. 2410, 2428-29 (1994)

Syrett, Harold C. et al, Editors; *The Founders' Constitution, Volume 1, Chapter 13, Document 38* **http://press-pubs.uchicago.edu/founders/documents/v1ch13s38.html**

Tansell, Charles C., Editor; **Documents Illustrative of the Formation of the Union of the American States** G.P,O, Washington 1927

Tarewell, Hon. Littleton W. and Clay, Henry biographers. **1 RA 86, et seq.** *Memoir of Author* (1852 edition)

Tarrey, R. B.: *Treasury Report on withdrawal of federal funds from the Bank of the United States*, **(1833)** 13 Has. Rep. 90

Taylor, Alan, **American Colonies: the Settling of North America,** Penguin Books, 2001.

The Book of Ranks and Dignities of British Society lately attributed in the press to Charles Lamb (1805) with an introduction by C.K. Shorter (Jonathan Cape Ltd., London 1924).

The University of Chicago Press. The Papers of Alexander Hamilton. 26 vols. New York and London: Columbia University Press, 1961–79

Thompson, E.P.**; Whigs and Hunters, the Origin of the Black Act** (Pantheon Books, 1975)

Thorp, Francis Newton, Editor; **Federal and State Constitutions Colonial Charters, and Other Organic Laws etc. (1909)**

Tiffany, Joel: **A Treatise on Government and Constitutional Law (1863)**

Tinniswood, Adrian:

http://www.nytimes.com/2010/07/04/opinion/04tinniswood.html?_r=0

Trumbach, Randolph; **The Rise of the Egalitarian Family, Aristocratic Kinship and Romantic Relations in Eighteenth Century England.** Studies in Social Discontinuity, Academic Press-, Inc., 1973

Van Buren, Martin; **Inquiry Into the Origin and Course of Political Parties in the United States** Editors: Abraham Van Buren John Van Buren Release Date: April 22, 2011 [EBook #35932]

Vassberg,David E.; **Land and Society in Golden Age Castile,(Cambridge Iberian and Latin American Studies)** Cambridge University Press (1984)

Voltaire, Francois-Marie Arouet de; **Candide of Optimism,** edited by Norman L. Torrey, 1946

Von Lowhen, Baron; **The Analysis of Nobility in its Origin With notes collected from the best English Antiquarians, and other Authors.** Printed and sold by J. Robinson, London 1754

Washington, H.A. Editor: **The Writings of Thomas Jefferson, New York : H.W. Derby, 1861**

Weisiger, Minor T., Compiler; *Northern Neck Land Proprietary Records* **Library of Virginia**

http://www.lva.virginia.gov/public/guides/rn23_nneckland.pdf

Williams, Basil; **The Whig Supremacy 1714-1760,** 2nd Edition (Clarendon Press 1974 Reprint)

Wilson, Charles; **England's Apprenticeship 1603-1763** (Longman Group Ltd. 1965, 1975 impression)

Winthrop, Fitz-John to Andrew Hamilton, Letter of June 9, 1698, Mass. Hist. Soc. Col., 5th series, IX

Wolf, Don M.; **The Leveler Manifestos of the Puritan Revolution** (T. Nelson and Sons, 1944)

Wood, Gordon S.:**The Radicalism of the American Revolution (1991)**

Wood, Gordon S.**; The Creation of the American Republic 1776-1787**

Woodhouse, A.S.P., Editor**; Puritanism and Liberty prefaced by Ivan Roots** (2nd ed. J.M. Dent & Sons Ltd. 1974)

Wright, Esmond**; Fabric of Freedom 1763-1800** (Hill & Wang 7th Printing 1968)

Zieber, Eugene; **Heraldry in America, 2nd ed.** (Bailey Banks & Biddle Co. Philadelphia 1909)

TABLE OF AUTHORITIES

STATUTES

CASES

OTHER AUTHORITIES

INDEX

xli